PASSIONATE JUSTICE:

A PROGRESSIVE MEMOIR IN ESSAYS

Jonathan Wolfman

Published by

The Educational Publisher Inc.
Biblio Publishing
BiblioPublishing.com

Library of Congress Number: 2013941594

ISBN: 978-1-62249-089-9

Photo by Ann Doshi

This book is dedicated to Tamar Weiss, my wife, and to my son, Graham Wolfman-Weiss, both of whom give my life its color and meaning and for whom my love and gratitude are boundless.

Acknowledgments

I present these essays in memory of my extraordinary parents, Zelda Bernstein Wolfman (1928-1973) and Bernard Wolfman (1924-2011); they made their passion for social justice my own.

And with abiding thanks to my brother, Brian Wolfman, and to my sister, Dina Baker. Two more supportive siblings simply cannot be found. And to Toni Wolfman, my father's brilliant, caring wife and partner from 1976 until he died.

I also wish to thank my students and colleagues from Akiba Hebrew Academy (Pennsylvania), Tianjin University (People's Republic of China), Hawaii Pacific University, Green Mountain Union High School (Vermont), Friends Select School (Pennsylvania), Torah Day

School of Atlanta, Bullis School (Maryland), and Chelsea School (Maryland).

A word of thanks, too, to my fellow 1963 Shoemaker Elementary (Elkins Park, Pennsylvania) and 1969 Cheltenham High (Cheltenham Township, Pennsylvania) graduates, and my other wonderful, earliest friends, many of whom I am grateful, still, to have.

I'm grateful as well for all the talented writers and readers at *Open Salon* and at *Our Salon,* two excellent websites for writers and readers.
I thank my editor, Elizabeth Langosy, for her advice and for her terrific editor's eye and ear. She is the executive editor at *Talking Writing,* a remarkable literary magazine.

I thank, too, Sheila Walsh, an immensely talented designer, for the cover of this book.

And to Liu Xiao-yi, finally found, and Zhang Ying, hoping to find her soon, again.

Contents

Introduction

Writing essays on social justice has been my daily passion and full-time work since 2008. To date, I've published roughly 1,500 pieces which have received excellent, helpful criticism from a group of longstanding, dear friends and from a consistent readership of fellow writers, first at *Open Salon* and subsequently at *Our Salon*. Some pieces have appeared on other sites, such as *Talking Writing*, *Does This Make Sense*, *Pal Talk News*, *The Jewish Reporter*, *Punchnel's*, *Beguile*, *Castle Gay Guide*, and *A World of Progress*. In early 2013, I began posting pieces readers have told me are their favorites every few months at the *Daily Kos*.

Because this book is a personal memoir that draws on social history, it reflects both general social history and my own. I respond in my writing to world and national events that have worked their way into my personal and professional life and informed my values and worldview. I've found that historical events and the justice inherent in them (or the lack thereof) continually resonate in the present.

Some of the essays included here address social justice issues I've confronted in my career as an ESL teacher in China and as a humanities teacher and public and private school administrator in the United States between 1973 and my retirement in 2007. Fundamental to all of my writing is a core of values that I ascribe to the rich history of Jewish social justice imperatives embodied in Deuteronomy 16:18, the eternal charge to the Hebrew clans as they move into the Land at the end of their forty years' trek: "Justice, justice shall you seek!" My mother and father made this mandate a part of their lives and, through their activities and commitment, offered it as a model to their children from my earliest days.

I've been convinced ever since my first readings in Plato that ideas and ideals preexist us and live on after us, which is why we can— with dedicated study and thoughtfulness—be fairly accurate in identifying instances when those standards come into play. The essays in this book show the development of my own sense of social justice, as well as global trends and the work that still needs to be done. And they demonstrate that this work goes on through individuals and institutions committed to alleviating injustice at all levels. While I see my social justice politics as nuanced and flexible, and while I think it's vital that we do our best to understand and learn from alternative views, my own politics are decidedly not relativist.

The pieces in this book are arranged chronologically with respect to my intellectual and emotional engagement with the events or experiences I describe. Since I understand justice to be an eternal idea—a sentient potential existing from the onset of time and living on after us—I see events, historical and personal, as justice's continual invitation to us to enact iterations of itself.

As such, the essay titles in the book are followed by one or a series of dates indicating not only the initial year I participated in or learned of an event but also subsequent years in which the story played out for me as a lesson in justice. In all cases, the final (or, occasionally, only) date is the year in which I wrote about the experience.

Thanks, in advance, for reading and, if you like, you may share your sense of these pieces with me. I'll be pleased to get back to you.

Jonathan Wolfman

JWolf41387@aol.com

Polio, Triumphant and Rejoicing

1956 - 2013

When I was very young, other children assumed that I'd had polio. I wore ungainly leg braces designed to remedy my (even now) rather hop-along gait, a result of having been born with Achilles tendons of variable lengths and a natural sense of balance akin to that of a fine drunk. It made for more medical conversation than my classmates likely wanted to hear—and for more than I'd ever wanted to rehearse over and again, anticipating new kids asking me at recess, "When did you get over polio?"

Yet, however repetitively annoying, it was not, in 1956, the absurd question it would be today on playgrounds everywhere—except in three nations: Pakistan, Afghanistan, and Nigeria.

Thanks to Drs. Salk and Sabin and to the ongoing efforts of the Bill and Melinda Gates Foundation and the World Health Organization, polio is nearly gone. Yet, in Muslim communities in those three nations, efforts to eradicate it have met with considerable resistance, some of it lethal and some of it going beyond superstition, a general aversion to the West, or concern about CIA activities in the region.

In December 2012, nine female polio workers were murdered in Pakistan. And while Near East and Central Asian Muslim aversion to vaccination predates the past decade—rumors have persisted there, for example, that vaccination is a CIA effort to spread AIDS and/or to make Muslim women infertile—the CIA's actual work in

3

the run-up to Osama bin Laden's killing was, for the Taliban and many other Muslims, dispositive.

However, reports Donald G. McNeil, Jr. in a February 2013 *New York Times* piece[1], "In its efforts to track Osama bin Laden, the [CIA] paid a Pakistani doctor to seek entry to bin Laden's compound on the pretext of vaccinating the children—presumably to get DNA samples as evidence that it was the right family."

Unsurprising, then, that polio workers haven't been greeted warmly in those communities for whom bin Laden was a hero, now a martyr. Until December, polio workers were not known to be targets. But on February 4, 2013, reports McNeil, Jr., at least nine polio workers were shot at two clinics in northern Nigeria. Most of the dead were women, shot in the back of the head. The militant Islamist group Boko Haram is suspected in the incident.

While I hope not to read of more such murders, I'm betting that I will—leaving not the West or reactionary elements within Islam but polio alone triumphant and rejoicing.

---

[1] Donald G. McNeil, Jr., "Gunmen Kill Nigerian Polio Vaccine Workers in Echo of Pakistan Attacks," *New York Times,* February 8, 2013.

Original Sin: Mississippi on My Mind & Heart

1957 - 2011

I feel, tonight, a little like Mr. Lincoln's House Divided. I am faced with two competing impulses, both of which I was born into and which were nurtured in me from the time I was a small child—when I fell asleep in bed many nights listening to civil rights news and rock and roll on my crystal radio. I particularly recall the nights spent pummeling a teddy bear, pretending it was Arkansas Governor Orville Faubus, who refused to allow Little Rock schools to integrate until Ike ordered in the Guard.

I saw tonight, almost by accident and yet again, segments of Ken Burn's *Civil War*, including those on the devastating Antietam battle in the early fall of 1862 and the Emancipation Proclamation effected the following New Year's Day. Then, again nearly by accident, I read of Mississippi's September 2011 decision, supported by Governor Haley Barbour, to sell $40,000,000 in tax-exempt bonds to build the Museum of Mississippi History and the Mississippi Civil Rights Museum.

Just a while back, Mr. Barbour said, to his myopic discredit, that he did not understand how others could have seen his state as a dangerous place to have been in the Civil Rights Era. In a December

2010 interview by Andrew Ferguson in *The Weekly Standard*[1], Barbour is quoted as saying, "I just don't remember it as being that bad."

Perhaps the man hasn't taken in what he should. His state was home to the 1955 murder of Chicago teen Emmet Till (for whistling at a white woman); the murder of NAACP activist Medgar Evers; the combined Klan/local police scheme to murder three young civil rights workers, Michael Schwerner, James Chaney, and Andrew Goodman; and countless more violations of human decency. Yet Mr. Barbour, lobbying his legislature hard for the museum projects, has little apparent ability to imagine that some, half a century back, may have found his home state frightening.

My conflict is this: On one hand, I have come to my early 60s largely unable—and possibly unwilling—to shake what I have come to realize is a nearly inborn disgust and utter distrust of Mississippi, both based on what the state symbolizes for me and despite what I know of it today. It now has, for example, more black elected officials than any other state. And yet, as a six-year-old, I listened to news at night and actively hated governors and other officials who stood at schoolhouse doors, mutely observing the horrors their fellow citizens were inflicting on the least of us.

On the other hand, I was taught—to a fault, perhaps—to see the good in people, as many people as possible and in as many ways as I could. This held as much for the bullies next door as it did for the racists who ran the South. This was not part of any religious mandate; it was what my parents taught through their own commitments and interpersonal behavior and through our dinner table conversations.

And so I read about Mr. Barbour and the museums he supports over the objections of many in both his party and the democratic

---

[1] Andrew Ferguson, "The Boy from Yazoo City," *The Weekly Standard,* December 27, 2010.

legislative minority, and I want to see good. I want to see it despite the fact that I wholly understand the economic and political motivations driving the man. I want to see if he continues to support the project after confirming that he won't be a candidate for the presidency. I want to see if his decision—even if based on motives that are mostly expedient—can serve to help redeem his own base instincts and those of his state and his region.

History's an Eel: Is "Six Million" Accurate?

1959 - 2013

I grew up quietly thinking that six million might be a low number. After all, I knew the killers' efficiency was such that the three million Jews who lived in Poland in 1939 had been reduced to 3,000 by 1945. Granted, the S.S. was particularly effective in Poland, but, I thought, if Nazis eliminated 99% of Polish Jewry in six years—and no serious historian disputes that—could we have accepted and then become wedded to numbers from other German-occupied nations that were simply too low, that didn't reflect the reality?

History's slippery.

When generations of well-read, well-meaning people accept numbers said to be accurate by so many chroniclers over so many decades—particularly when those numbers are attached to the attempted destruction of a people and their history—the numbers themselves become as tenacious as Jew-hunters and adhere to our consciousness in ways that tend to defy challenge. Depending on the direction of the attempted recalculations (even if evidence driven), moral authority can attach to the original numbers and moral outrage to proposed revisions.

It now turns out that the chroniclers and researchers of the Final Solution may have, from the earliest post-war years, dramatically miscalculated the numbers; generations after ours may well renounce our six million in favor of an even more awful reality. That's the conclusion of recent research by scholars at the United States Holocaust Memorial Museum.

Researchers at the museum's Center for Advanced Holocaust Studies compiled statistics on S.S.-run camps and ghettos in a multi-volume encyclopedia[2] published by the Indiana University Press in association with the museum.

As related in a March 2013 *New York Times* article[3] by Eric Lichtblau, a visiting scholar at the museum, the encyclopedia catalogs thousands of sites, providing a more comprehensive history than was ever available before of the "living and working conditions, activities of the Jewish councils, Jewish responses to persecution, demographic changes, and details of the liquidation of the ghettos." Maps of the sites are included.

The researchers, led by Dr. Geoffrey Megargee, have found that there may well have been over 42,500 S.S.-run camps and ghettos during the twelve years of the Third Reich. These sites, the researchers say, imprisoned, enslaved, and/or murdered between fifteen and twenty million Jews.

To be sure, these scholars are not the first to have suggested that the numbers "history" settled on before many of us were born—and then reinforced in us as children and as adults—may have been low. Still, this new body of research appears to be the most detailed and comprehensive verification of this claim to date.

If there were, as now seems quite possible, at least 42,500 sites, the destruction of European Jewry would then appear to have come far

---

[2] http://www.ushmm.org/research/center/encyclopedia/about/
[3] Eric Lichtblau, "The Holocaust Just Got More Shocking," *New York Times,* March 1, 2013.

closer than we'd realized to Hitler's goal of making Europe *Judenrein*.

A reason I love reading history, loved teaching history and the literature emerging from it, love writing about both, is precisely because history is this slippery. It's an eel. If you can comfortably live with the idea that ambiguity can intrude at any time into what has been seen as settled, as undisputed, I think you're a richer person for it, and we're a richer culture for your lithe and resilient intellect and heart.

Mazal Tov.

Beating Hell Out of Johnny's Bully, Then Mine

1960 - 1963 - 2010

I understand what happens when schools and neighborhoods cave to bullies and their parents. I understand the months-long group bullying at South Hadley High School in western Massachusetts that left the pretty "new girl" dead by her own hand in January 2010. And I understand all the horrid, relentless school-based incidents that result in gay kids' suicides.

As a teacher and administrator for 36 years in both private and public schools, I was fairly successful at handling bullies, both boys and girls, and their too-often morally deranged parents. The attackers were children whose emotional wreckage was visible even before reading the thick files that accompanied them. They wore their signature distress in their frightened sneers, on scraped knuckles, on flashing teeth. Yet, as rotten and vicious as their disgraceful behavior may have been, these were, at bottom, kids, and I nearly always understood—or, with colleagues, discovered— the genesis of their often inchoate rage, rage that must, every day, find release.

I was in the first grade when I first stood up for a bullied kid. I was in the play yard on a windy fall day at Shoemaker Elementary School in Elkins Park, Pennsylvania, just north of Philadelphia. The concrete-and-macadam fenced-in yard seemed to us enormous and

11

inescapable; moat-like, it wrapped around three sides of the old stonework school.

I'd been teased myself—particularly by an older neighbor boy, Stevie—because I'd worn leg braces until the summer after kindergarten, and so I knew what the sting felt like. But I was lucky: I was also pals with the most popular boys in our class, so it fast became uncool to go after me. I may have been a gimp, but I was "their" gimp, my class's gimp, and by first grade I was picked (however ruefully, given my typically detrimental effect on final scores) for recess football and pimple ball squads and relay races. I was allowed, on occasion, to "win" a relay race. That's how it is if you've got a minor disability and your best friend is popular and he sees past your lack of physical grace. I'm grateful to him (and the others) even today.

But Johnny Sparks didn't have that support.

Johnny was huge (although not fat), a bit clumsy, and not yet socially articulate. He certainly hadn't a clue that the best way to deal with bullies was to smack one very hard on the mouth, in view of their bully pals, the second the taunting began. He just took it. We all knew the signs immediately prior to his—to anyone's—victimization and so did our teachers, who routinely vanished when the taunting started.

On this leafy, windy day, they cornered Johnny Sparks by the fence, maybe twenty boys. They were all smaller than he, but it didn't matter and they knew it. They seemed particularly bent that day on nailing him. I'd watched him being teased often; I knew my position of grace, and I wasn't keen to undermine it.

Yet, something in me snapped that morning, and I can't say why. The taunting was only slightly more awful that day, but perhaps it had an edge of real violence. I moved in front of Johnny, between him and the gang. I yelled as loud as a first grader can at the lead bully, a third or fourth grader called Billy. I told him he was a damned bastard, they all were damned bastards, and if they didn't

12

leave right now, I'd beat the hell out of Tim (the littlest bully), beat him very, very bloody, as soon as I had the shot, publicly or no.

This, of course, was uproarious entertainment for the gang, who laughed derisively and joked about my old leg braces.

All sense left me. I limped over, not to Tim but to much-larger Billy, and punched him as hard as I could, smash on the nose and smash on the mouth. Blood whooshed in cascades over his lips, down his chin, onto his shirt and onto mine. Blood came and came and so did the school bell, ringing us in from the yard. The idiots scattered. I was deliriously pleased with myself.

Back inside the classroom, though, I felt increasingly worried, sure I was going to get it and bad on the uphill walk home from school.

Nothing happened. Nothing. That taught me something: If you stand up to bullies, surprise them, denounce them for the cowards they are, if you use your fists, even ones weaker than theirs, you may shock them into turning back into little boys. It can happen.

The blood helps.

The historian/philosopher Hannah Arendt pointed out in her still-controversial 1962 book about the trial of Adolf Eichmann, *Eichmann in Jerusalem*, that in towns where Jewish leaders resisted and, in some cases, outright refused orders from the S.S. to turn over citizen lists, survival rates were often much higher than in places where Jewish leaders readily complied. That makes sense, if only because it gave Jews who were inclined to flee the time to do so. Even the lethal work of world-class bullies can, albeit rarely, be delayed or blunted by shocking them with your resistance. Writ small, it can happen in schoolyards, too.

And in backyards.

Some time after rescuing Johnny Sparks, I took a brick to the forehead of the neighbor boy, Stevie, as he and I tensely crouched

13

on either side of the green sticker bush hedge separating his family's backyard from mine. The schoolyard incident told me I needn't take this third grader's taunts and abuse one year, one day, one moment more. Stevie's forehead opened up, and so did my world.

It's not always that simple, of course, and I taught my students and my son that violence is rarely a justifiable first option. Yet, I do not swallow the lie that bullying is hard to discern and too complex to bring down.

We all knew; we all know. Most are afraid to act. Schoolteachers and administrators who turn from the pain suffered by Johnny Sparks and that girl in Massachusetts and the gay kids driven to suicide should be subject to criminal sanctions. I'd be even more pleased if the parents of bullies were subject to stiff fines, if not to prison in many cases, because they also know. They always know.

My Son and I and the Freedom Riders' 50th Anniversary

1961 - 2011

My son, 22, is a black man; naive would be the very least adjective to suit him. When he was first allowed to go to the mall with his crowd—his remarkably mixed, integrated, suburban crowd of white, Latino, Asian, and other black youngsters—I didn't need to tell him, though I did, that he might be shadowed by the (usually minority) mall cops and that many of his pals wouldn't. He knew, too, well before he got his license, what driving-while-black means; he took his older friends' experiences to heart. And yet he took as natural that his circle was as integrated as it was and is and that it felt and still feels so natural. And, of course, it is; it should.

So it's ironic when I mention to him one morning (in a tone of reverence he's come to know so well) that it is the fiftieth anniversary of the Freedom Riders setting out from Washington, D.C., not far from where we live now. That he knows what awaited those first incredibly brave souls on buses, at lunch counters, in shops, near polling booths—that he truly understands in salient ways what he's learned from us and from books—doesn't stop him from wondering aloud why my tone becomes as reverential as it does, why my Muhammad Ali "Impossible Is Nothing" poster dominates my office space, and why, at times, I well up when I hear Dr. King's magnificent cadences in President Obama's voice.

What he does know is that the horrid and sustained Klan violence that met those Riders, the viciousness that killed Viola Liuzzo and Medgar Evers, the evil that murdered four small black girls in that Birmingham church basement were part of a larger reign of terror, with fifty bombs directed against people with my son's skin color in Birmingham that month alone.

And yet he also knows that he lives in a changed world from the one I lived as a teen. So when he tells me, "Dad. Please. Relax." when he hears my voice begin to crack as we discuss these issues, I do try. And I wonder. I wonder if he and I will ever bridge this wonderful, horrible gap.

Want to Get Away with Murder? Don't Kill a White Guy

1962 - 2010

I first thought about capital punishment when I was very young and heard stories of the Sacco and Vanzetti trial, Southern mob lynchings of blacks, and the sensational trial and 1962 execution of convicted Philadelphia killer Elmo Smith, the last man sentenced to death in my home state.

Over time—and this surprises me somewhat, given my tendency to see many sides of issues (perhaps too many, I've been told)—I've become an absolutist as to capital punishment. Many a student has offered me chances to bend a bit and concur that the death penalty has a place in a mature, civil culture. Hitler has been a popular prod, as has the perennial question "What if it were your child who had been murdered?" I've disappointed them, sometimes sharply so when I've taught at Jewish day schools. There is simply no circumstance under which I can imagine supporting capital punishment. While I could cite many reasons, one will do here.

A fact about murder trials that tends to startle people is that juries across the country are more likely to dish death when a murder victim is white, no matter the race of the killer. That is, you're far more likely to die yourself if you kill a white person—regardless of whether you are white, black, Latino, or Asian—than if you kill a black, Latino, or Asian.

17

To put it another way, if you commit murder, your own race is less likely to determine whether or not you die than is the race of your victim.

A 2011 report from the Death Penalty Information Center, "Struck by Lightning,"[4] shows that the overall rate by which juries and judges mete out death has declined dramatically—a positive step, in my view.

In 1994, 328 people were given the death penalty nationally; in 2008, the number was 111, a decrease of two-thirds. The trend appears to be continuing. It can be seen most starkly, and perhaps most surprisingly, in Texas, where the greatest decline has occurred in the number of juries giving the death sentence. The Lone Star State executed 9 people in 2011; in the 1990s, Texas averaged 34 executions each year. Researchers ascribe the decline, in part, to the increasing skepticism of juries about the decency and efficacy of capital punishment.

And yet juries—and this holds for all-white as well as mixed-race juries—appear over and again to prize white lives more than they cherish minority lives. While sad, this shouldn't be surprising. We know that, everywhere, traditionally marginalized and victimized minorities often and unwittingly internalize majority-culture biases. Not much else could reasonably explain why juries of all racial makeups consistently punish with the death penalty killers of white people so much more often than those who murder people of other races.

Unless and until that paradigm is upended, I cannot see reasonable people even considering support for capital punishment.

---

[4] http://www.deathpenaltyinfo.org/documents/StruckByLightning.pdf

MAD Magazine, Civil Liberties, and a Third Grade Subversive

1959 - 1963 - 2011

When I hear about the successful efforts of The American Civil Liberties Union (ACLU) and hundreds of other, smaller, regional organizations to halt some of the most egregious attempts to restrict constitutional rights, I'm put in mind of sitting three rows behind Bobby B. in third grade. I think of Bobby opening his public school-issued King James Version on our teacher's cue, unfolding his wider-than-the-KJV *MAD Magazine*, treating us to his devil-may-care laughter, and showing his pint-sized stoicism at being immediately yanked from class to wait on the bench outside the principal's office. On those days, Bobby B. was my hero.

Sometimes, those of us committed to the politics of individual freedom buy into the dominant media thrust about Who's Winning. That thrust hasn't been about civil liberties in quite some time. What has largely been lost in the continuous assault on individual rights— and the messaging about it that has swept from statehouse to statehouse and has infected Congress since late 2010—are the stories of how much freedom has been preserved and fought for, how much wrong has been stopped.

While they may not make the same headlines as the forces of reaction, there have been significant victories in this era and in earlier times that we must be aware of and celebrate. The following cases, all but one resolved in 2011, were published in the Summer

2011 edition of *Civil Liberties,* the ACLU national newsletter, within an article titled "Defending Freedom, Statehouse by Statehouse."

- Fourteen states have passed laws based on the Support Our Law Enforcement and Safe Neighborhoods Act, the Arizona anti-illegal immigration measure widely known as Arizona Senate Bill 1070. However, various efforts to enforce it have failed due to ACLU lawsuits. In one case, Jim Shee, an Arizona citizen of Chinese and Spanish heritage, was detained while driving to his seventieth birthday party. He was not violating any law, traffic or otherwise. The police nonetheless demanded to see "his papers." This happened to Mr. Shee again within days. The ACLU took on Mr. Shee's case under the suspicion that his only crime was driving-while-brown in Arizona. In another case, a Georgia man named Paul Edwards was arrested for driving an illegal immigrant to a hospital emergency room. A churchgoer, Mr. Edwards said that it was worth it to him to risk fines and/or imprisonment in order to fulfill his "Christian duty" to aid someone in need.

- ACLU (and other) lobbying has prevented the state of South Carolina from making it possible for doctors and insurers to refuse to discuss with patients abortion as an option. The ACLU pointed out that, first, abortion is legal and, second, that both doctors and insurers are licensed by the state and so must adhere to law.

- The organization is trying to prevent the states of Rhode Island and Washington from allowing pharmacists to refuse to fill birth control prescriptions. The ACLU's position is that birth control is legal; pharmacists are also state-licensed and must follow the law.

- The ACLU is making headway in a challenge to an Arizona law that allows public university counseling centers to deny all services to gay and lesbian students.

- The ACLU was instrumental in lobbying for the end of "Don't Ask/Don't Tell."

- The organization has been a prime mover in lobbying the federal government to stop its enforcement of the discriminatory Defense of Marriage Act. It continues to push Congress to overturn it.

- The ACLU won a landmark, yet little-known, federal case in which it was ruled illegal for private corporations to patent human breast cancer and ovarian cancer genes. The win has forced a legal review of similar patents dating back to the 1980s.

- The ACLU's suit was critical in the 2003 demise of U.S. laws that had previously made sexual intimacy between same-sex partners crimes in themselves. Numerous jurisdictions had continued to arrest and prosecute people under these laws until Supreme Court Justice Anthony Kennedy's majority opinion in *Lawrence v. Texas* invalidated antisodomy laws nationwide.

These are just eight cases. There have been hundreds more. Thousands.

I vividly recall when the Schempp family, my neighbors just a township over in Abington, Pennsylvania, won their landmark Supreme Court case. From that day in 1963, public school children of any religion—or of no religion—could no longer be held captive to daily Bible readings.

I have to say, too, that I'm proud my father worked on that case. This, and similar ACLU cases, made a mark on me as a child.

I have no idea where Bobby B. is now, but I'd like to think, were he to read this, he'd nod, smile, and pass me his copy of that *MAD*.

How We Speak and Write:
The Language of Equality

1965 - 2012

It's fascinating how a desire to corner the market on language enters cultural change dialogue. It speaks to the power of words to shape realities.

Many will, for example, recall the debate and, at times, the rancor over who rightly got to use the word "black" forty or fifty years back. There had been, before "black" became standard usage, some feeling that only African-Americans who were on or supporting the front lines of change could rightly claim the term.

To cite another example, in my community, there have always been those who insist on "Jewish-American," finding "American Jew," if not offensive, less preferred, suggesting a misplaced emphasis. There are numbers of American Jews, in fact, who object strenuously to "Jew" and much prefer the adjectival identifier "Jewish." While I have no issue with "Jew," I understand the historical reasons (*Juden!*) for the sensitivities involved.

Similar language issues surround the changing legal status of gay citizens.

The tremendous win for marriage equality in New York —New York! our financial and cultural hub!—and a piece I wrote about it at the time spurred a series of discussions among my friends and family, some of which I'd like to share.

As I've written in numerous pieces, I am clear that marriage equality—political and economic equality for gay citizens—is the civil rights mandate of this generation. Just as Lerone Bennett, Jr. said in "The White Problem in America," the August 1965 *Ebony* cover article that upended the then typical view of race, there is in America a problem, vast and deep. But now it is a heterosexual one.

I believe the gay activist movement's increasing focus on marriage equality is the right tack; the right to marry is the core of equal social status. It's about equality in the full range of family-law issues: fair and just taxation, housing, public accommodations, workplace rights, and medical access.

Everyone with whom I've discussed these issues both prior and subsequent to the June 2011 vote at Albany agrees that the New York legislature made the right decision to pass the Marriage Equality Act. Several, however, also believe that as gay citizens gain the right to marry in more and more jurisdictions, a new term for marriage between heterosexuals should be found to distinguish their legal matrimonial bond from that of gay couples.

I could not disagree more.

Language is socially potent—so powerful, in fact, that we rarely pause to consider it. Promulgating a new term for the union of straight couples would inevitably harm gay couples and undermine the gains for which they've struggled. Whatever new name heterosexuals might claim would soon be seen as somehow better, describing the correct, preferred bond. It would quickly bring gays back to a lesser status.

The idea that we need a separate term (instead of happily sharing "marriage") strikes me in another way. I think it reawakens for some the question of whether being gay is a choice. If it were universally accepted that being gay is simply about who one is, there would be far fewer voices raising concern about who gets to use the term "marriage." The answer is not simply, "'Marriage' has always been used this way." Although true, this response is next to meaningless

24

when stacked against the fundamental human and citizenship rights of gay Americans to enjoy the same social, political, and economic benefits as married straight couples—and racial and religious minorities.

To entertain the idea, even passingly, that being gay is more of a choice than, say, being black, a person would also have to harbor the idea that gay people everywhere choose and have always chosen to live lives of grinding, degrading discrimination and social disapprobation. And that just makes no sense.

The marriage equality struggle moves forward, in state legislatures (and many states have constitutional provisions forbidding it) and through state and federal courts (where I do think Fourteenth Amendment Equal Protection arguments have real legs). New York may prove to be a turning point; we'll soon know where this leads. However it progresses (and it will progress), we should not lose sight of the language issues. Being continually aware of language biases inherent in this and in other social sea changes leads us toward more just outcomes.

Skepticism, Cynicism, and Just Wars

1968 - 2011

(First published in slightly different form in *Does This Make Sense?*)

Now, in 2011, that we're in a Near East war for the third time in a decade—having engaged combat in Afghanistan, Iraq, and Libya—an old, persistent thought gnaws at me anew. Those of us born immediately after the Second War— the baby boomers—have never known a war that shows us with immediacy and conviction that there are conflicts both moral and necessary. And yet we've lived in an America at war, if we consider Vietnam a starting point, about half the time we've been alive.

Until the Towers went down, I could argue that no time was spent in ethical military endeavor. Even the rightness of the efforts to stop Al Qaeda were sullied for many by our overtly ill-conceived war in Iraq, and, many agree, in Afghanistan. And yet I'm convinced the war to stop Al Qaeda is just.

The Southeast Asian war left my generation deeply cynical about overseas military engagement. I deeply appreciate and admire thoughtful, healthy skepticism, and yet I wonder if many in my generation distinguish between skepticism and cynicism readily enough.

As I see the distinction, a skeptic, believing everything is possible on the continuum between good and evil, questions hard and works hard to get policies right. A cynic, however, has come to believe that the fix is in and so rarely believes social action matters, that sustained good isn't really possible.

For many in my generation, the line between skepticism and cynicism has, perhaps, been blurred by our experiences. I wonder if we've been rendered ambivalent, to varying degrees, by our nation's moral and strategic failures in Korea, Cuba, Vietnam, Laos, Cambodia, Nicaragua, Iraq, and Afghanistan. We've seen our military engage so often and so harmfully, that it has become tough to recognize what a necessary and moral war looks like.

The effort to end Al Qaeda is, for me, a clear moral necessity. I do think the recent revolutions in North Africa, particularly in Egypt, speak to Al Qaeda's undoing in the long term. However, I think we need to continue our own war against Al Qaeda, however shadowy the terrorist organization may be and however muddied our foreign policy has been since the World War II.

Whatever else Vietnam did, whatever else the murdering of young, civilian protesters at Jackson State and at Kent State did, they undermined the willingness of many in my generation to gauge and engage foreign policy issues, particularly military ones, with an appropriate amount of subtlety, nuance, and healthy skepticism.

The Meteor, The Whale, Hubris, and Awe

1969 - 2013

Odd, perhaps, to apprehend the yellow-white-hot streaking ball. Is there some comic-cosmic rule that meteors *have* to, absolutely *have* to plummet into frozen Siberian lakes? Why not, say, Bloomington, Minnesota's Mall of America (at 3:00 a.m., of course)?

What's 44 years in meteor time? Odd, too, that the meteor put me singularly in mind of my 1969 fall term as a Penn freshman, when English professor, nineteenth-century American Gothic and Poe scholar (and then president of the Poe Society), rail-thin, six-foot-six Benjamin Franklin Fisher IV—honest—made his off-hand, first-day-of-class remark that the fifty or so of us would be, to his delight, whittled to twenty or, better yet, to fifteen, by his first assignment: "You shall read and know *Moby Dick*, all 599 pages, and in addition, ladies and gentlemen, you shall come prepared a week hence to thrall me, I say again, to thrall me. You, whomever I choose—and I will choose numbers of you from whoever's left—will discuss, based on a paper you shall type, your thorough understanding of Ahab's sin, his true evil."

Yes, the Siberian hot rock put me in mind of Professor Fisher's challenge, to which perhaps eight others and I rose, to his glee. He actually danced a brief jig when he saw how few we now were.

I am not an astronomer; I graduated only because in those years Penn's science requirement could be satisfied by psych courses. I am

28

not a scientist, but my literature studies taught me awe for nature and for the Platonic Who—who just may lurk above and behind the natural world. Perhaps this sounds quaint, but, yes, those lit courses did teach me that.

And what I know is that Ahab's evil is our collective original sin. We believe we are the Who that lurks above and behind the natural world, and we dance and jig through our lives, making for ourselves an infant's hubristic celebration of *our* intelligence, *our* wisdom, *our* dignity, *our* power, and our pathetically weak bid for control—as Ahab did, despite the continuous, deadening thud of his whale-chewed wooden leg, which ought to have reminded him, but of course did not, of the whale's, of Nature's, and of the Who's ultimate control.

We really ought to recognize and perhaps say aloud what Ahab would not—say it aloud at least every so often, such as when, from above and behind, eleven-ton chunks of galactic rock visit us—that killing the white whale, particularly for something as small and venal as revenge, ought to be beneath us, and that the only proper human posture is awe.

The Fetus from Milpitas

1973 - 2011

From our infancy in the early 1950s, Randy and I grew up together in a Philadelphia duplex. Our moms were closest friends and remained so until each of them died from unusually rare (and different) debilitating cancers, my mom in 1973 and Randy's some time later. It was said that our mothers took us out together in our strollers several times a day, and we grew—as toddlers, tweens, and teens—continually in one another's presence. We enjoyed the same stuff: *MAD Magazine, Twilight Zone, American Bandstand,* Victor Mature's awful gladiator movies, Lenny Bruce, doo-wop, baseball.

Randy and I shared a bent for dark and absurd, socially subversive humor and for torturing our mothers. Our humor, at its worst, included terrible pranks, for which we typically enjoyed just and miserable punishment—separately and for eons. One prank found Randy's mom brushing her teeth with Brylcreem ("A Little Dab'll Do Ya*")*.

A far worse one involved the decapitation of two dolls belonging to his sister, Denise. We were then six or seven and stunned that no one else saw the humor. Randy was even more stunned when his answer to our mothers' thunderous and scowl-laden "Why?"—"But it's *Denise*!" —didn't result in the instant maternal understanding we'd expected. Randy found himself having to work off the cost of new Chatty Cathy and Betsy Wetsy dolls. I was barred from outdoor play for a hundred years.

As we grew, we shared similar tastes and penchants, as twins might, particularly for seeing bizarre humor in nearly everything, although we never again took such terrible paths of destruction. The worst we ever did after that wreckage at Denise's expense was, at eighteen, to return our draft cards to the well-intended people who had sent them to us. Our parents may have been silently proud, but, vocally, they were not altogether pleased.

After college, we both went to the Bay Area where Randy stayed on in various neighborhoods and jobs. Today he works as an industrial film producer and lives with his family in Marin. I returned home to take a position teaching humanities in a Jewish day school. We've never lost touch, and we visit each other when we're able. We are, in a wondrous way, still best friends.

Randy made up his mind to stay in California in the year *Roe v. Wade* was decided. He was determined to do anything that would keep him there until he could use his Boston University film degree to earn a living, so at 22, he took menial work in a San Francisco hospital.

As low man, it fell to Randy to carry sawed-off and bagged limbs and extracted, necrotic kidneys from operating rooms to storage. State law at the time required tagging and storing everything that became separated from a patient.

Including fetuses.

One summer day, as on many days subsequent to *Roe*, organized protests occurred at hospitals where abortions were known to take place. At Randy's workplace, that day's protest started just after noon and by 3:00 swelled to several hundred people, mostly women carrying signs—such as "Milpitas Moms for Life"—and a dozen or so pastors.

By 2:30, the TV people were taping and interviewing, though Randy didn't know it.

31

That's when his supervisor told him they were out of the nondescript jars typically used for fetus storage. Handing him a tray of what looked for all the world like relabeled and sterilized Gerber jars (because they were), he told Randy to cross the campus and check into refrigeration perhaps a dozen fetuses. To do that, he'd have to cross an open quad—the demonstration site.

As Randy made his way across the quad, three demonstrators rushed up to ask his opinion about the recent Court decision. It would have been quite a coup, he later realized, for them to get a supportive sound bite from a hospital employee. When they saw that Randy carried a tray of what appeared to be baby food jars, they gushed and swooned, calling over a cameraman.

Before Randy knew what was happening, a microphone was in his face and a man was asking what he thought of the demonstrators and the Court's holding. An enthusiastic woman pointed to the jars as evidence of Randy's obvious goodwill toward the Cause.

The TV man asked Randy, "What do you have there, son?"

Randy didn't skip a beat. "We're making a spaghetti western here, sir," he said, smiling into the camera. "*The Fetus from Milpitas*."

Bless the lad. My oldest and still-dearest friend Randy was back to pounding the pavement by evening.

Why I Invited a Neo-Nazi to a Jewish Sleep-Away Camp

1977 - 2011

(Originally published in *Punchnel's*)

By the 1970s, it was likely that nearly every Jewish child in America had had an opportunity to meet and question—at school, synagogue, YMHA—a Holocaust survivor, whether of Auschwitz, Belzec, or Sobibor or whether taken in and protected by incredibly brave Christians. I recall when I first arranged for a survivor to speak at Akiba Hebrew Academy, where I taught humanities. I was 23. I collected Mrs. Grubmann, then in her late seventies, at her home, and as we turned onto the campus road, she quite deliberately pushed up the sleeves on her thin, steel-grey cardigan. The tattooed numbers slapped me so hard my hands jumped from the wheel. In English still heavily inflected with German, she said, "Young man, please be alert." Then, softly: "I know. You've never seen one before; it's all right."

And now, with the very last of the survivors dying out, children of all backgrounds have video and other archives and museums available to them. As horrible as a child may initially feel, they need to confront mass murder. And yet they don't, typically, get a chance to confront mass murderers themselves—or, at least, their ideas and feelings in the person of a neo-Nazi.

I provided that opportunity for about 700 kids in the summer of 1977, at a Jewish sleep-away camp not too far northwest of Philadelphia.

33

I was hired as the camp's drama director, and we put on some terrific productions. We made a film of *The Golem*, the original Frankenstein's monster story, if you will, and we staged a moving production of the Yiddish classic, *The Dybbuk*, a nineteenth-century tale of mysticism wherein a man's spirit inhabits the body of his beloved after he dies in order to keep her from an arranged marriage to a man she does not love.

On the strength of those successes, I approached the camp director with my neo-Nazi idea. He and I were similar, edgy, push-the boundaries-souls, and he signed on immediately.

In the run-up to the evening's event, we posted unsavory but not lurid Holocaust flyers throughout the camp, announcing a short film and a speaker. There didn't seem to be a great deal of interest; after all, these were Jewish kids, mostly teens who feigned or genuinely felt an oh-no-not-this-again apathy. They'd heard it all before.

There was a defensive, dismissive buzz as the kids came into the dining hall. We showed a clip from a documentary short, one that, while honest, wasn't too graphic. Once the film had finished, I stepped to the front and introduced our guest amidst the summertime evening teenage chatter.

"Our guest, Hans—he won't give us his last name—has agreed to share with you the program of his organization, the American Nazi Party. My expectation is that no matter what you hear in the next half hour, you will be respectful and save questions for the end."

There were a few giggles as well as some deliberately outsized gasps. I then motioned for our guest to step out from the kitchen and join me at the dais. The man, in his late twenties, was well over six feet, perhaps 190 pounds. His uniform alone was enough to hush kids fast. The swastikas made even me slightly uncomfortable; I wondered if I'd done the right thing. I felt a tiny twinge of regret as I saw some of our youngest children, the eight- and nine-year-olds, ball themselves up in their seats.

Hans's light-brown hair was close cropped but not buzzed; his eyes were green, his jackboots shiny black. There was a slight rumble from the oldest campers in the back of the room, but many of them were my drama kids, and they settled in when I shot them a look. I took a seat.

Hans opened, reading from a sheet of paper.

"You Jews," he sneered. "Over centuries, you amassed enough wealth to begin to control banking in Europe and what we now call mass communications, and you used your wealth to systematically deny the Aryan peoples their God-given right to exercise their will and power over inferior peoples and races."

In case anyone in the now-stupefied audience had missed a note of the initial venom, Hans repeated the opener, then launched into a fifteen-minute justification of the Holocaust—*had it ever truly occurred.* The children needed to understand, Hans said, that Jewish-owned newspaper and radio corporations had swelled a few thousand deaths of a few thousand unruly prisoners of war into something not only wholly untrue but—*had it happened*—it would have been necessary in order to return Europe to its original, rightful rule.

By this point, several counselors had begun moving to take their kids from the hall, but the director, a very sharp-eyed guy, went to each of them individually, bent his head, and said a few words, and those counselors indicated by their body language that everyone in their charge was to stay.

Hans then spoke of how Jews are responsible for pretty much all of America's current and recent ills, from pornography, propping up the "criminal" Martin Luther King, "forcing Israel onto the world," the Chicago Convention Riots of 1968, the Supreme Court decision on abortion just four years earlier, and the "utter license and lewdness" in film and on television to the movement to confiscate guns from law-abiding citizens, the "illegal 1972 presidential campaign" of black New York Congresswoman Shirley Chisholm, the Court's decision fourteen years earlier to "kick my Bible out of our schools", and the filling of the nation's public school classrooms with "Jew teachers straight from Jew-run universities."

After twenty minutes of this and more, Hans shared his solution: "Since this is really a problem about race and about how inferior races think and scheme, our plan is to take the so-called 'African-Americans' and the Jews and other people who are inferior by blood and place them in camps like those used in California for the Japs thirty years ago. Even your own Jew-President, *Rosenfelt*, had the sense to do that in a time of war. We are still at war."

He stopped, waiting for applause that never came. He sat down at a chair near the lectern. The room was hushed. I moved to the podium and asked if there were questions. I looked out over 700 faces. I think, honestly, that some children had aged perceptibly in that time. I was more than nervous.

A counselor, Judy, stood and in a small but clearly outraged voice said, "Jon, how could you?" She turned to our director. "And *you*? How in God's *name*...?"

I recall how shaky my knees were, but my voice, I'm grateful, was firm. I said, "Judy. Everyone. You know, in not too long a time, there will be no more Holocaust survivors. There won't be opportunities for us to meet with them, nor with the kind of men who perpetrated those crimes. Some of those crimes were committed against your families."

I paused, and then explained, "In the winter, I act in a group at Allen's Lane Theater Company, in Philadelphia. Hans is also an actor in our group at Allen's Lane. He's actually a Jewish man named Jerry Goldberg, and he and I and your camp director thought this would be something you would remember and tell your families about. And, if we're lucky, it will stick with you in a good way, in a way that will feel better than some of you feel right now. Some of you will have kids of your own within ten years, you know."

36

I invited Jerry to say a few words, as himself.

To my knowledge—and remarkably—not one family lodged a complaint. In any case, I was back next season. And here's teaching's delicious irony: About fifteen years later, a woman approached me in a multiplex lobby. She was holding the hand of a little boy, perhaps five or six.

"Are you Mr. Wolfman?" she asked. "You're Jon Wolfman. You directed me in that camp play about the man's ghost."

I smiled at her. "*The Dybbuk,* an old, Yiddish play." I placed her face but not her name.

"Yes! And I was there the night you...."

"The 'Nazi.'"

"Yes." Her face darkened. "Him. I hated you for that, a long time. Years later, I even told my husband how much I hated what you did. But when we had Noah, I thought about it, what you did." Her face changed, brightened some. "And I'm going to tell him someday."

The Passage Owns Me
1977 (the first year I taught Huck) - 2011

(Originally published in somewhat different form in *Beguile)*

For all of us who love to read, there are quiet, gorgeous, or supernova passages that do not simply linger but work their way into muscle and bone and become as much a part of who we are, years and decades on, as they were a part of the writer. They can, even upon a return reading decades on, provide a peace that, as T.S. Eliot said in the final passage of *The Wasteland,* goes beyond human understanding, washing over and into our pores, cells, and souls as an enduring tonic like no other.

There are passages, paragraphs, even just sentences in Virginia Woolf (the ending sentences in *To The Lighthouse*), William Faulkner (the opening sentence of a hundred-plus words defining inner time and space, in *Absalom, Absalom!*), or Thomas Mann (the sequences on love and honor in *The Magic Mountain*) —and so many others—that work on me in this way.

These and hundreds of others have stayed in me for so many years. I won't list more now because I'm concerned (foolishly, I know) about a lack of inclusion. But I must note one more, one that has lodged in my heart and in my mind like no other, a paragraph that originated with Samuel Clemens but that I have come to feel, in a strange and wondrous way, that I now own and that my soul will own long after I pass.

Midway, Chapter 31, *Adventures of Huckleberry Finn:* Huck's crisis of conscience, the conscience of a child but also the emerging,

38

battered conscience of a deeply evil—evil because chosen—national racial history mirrored in that small boy. He has one chance to wrest himself from the stranglehold of nefarious criminals, and he can do it by denouncing Jim to Miss Watson, Jim's owner under law—Jim the runaway, now a man to Huck, no longer a slave only:

> "Miss Watson your runaway nigger Jim is down here two mile below Pikesville and Mr. Phelps has got him and he will give him up for the reward if you send. HUCK FINN

> "I felt good and all washed clean of sin for the first time I had ever felt so in my life, and I knowed I could pray now....I went on thinking...how near I come to being lost and going to hell. And got to thinking over our trip down the river; and I see Jim before me, all the time; in the day, and in the night-time, sometimes moonlight, sometimes storms, and we a floating along, talking, and singing, and laughing. But somehow I couldn't seem to strike no places to harden me against him, but only the other kind. I'd see him standing my watch on top of his'n...so I could go on sleeping; and see...how good he always was; ...and then I happened to look around, and see that paper.

> "It was a close place. I took it up, and held it in my hand. I was a-trembling, because I'd got to decide, forever, betwixt two things, and I knowed it. I studied a minute, sort of holding my breath, and then says to myself: 'All right, then, I'll go to hell'- and tore it up."[5]

This electrifying passage subverts all traditional American social and religious imperatives and demands that our country grow up and adhere to higher law. I've said that I have come to believe I own this passage; the truth is that it owns me.

---

[5] Mark Twain, *Adventures of Huckleberry Finn* (Chatto & Windus, 1884; Charles L. Webster and Company, 1885).

Imprisoned for Their Poverty: Irish Boys in America, Irish Girls in Northern Ireland

1977 - 2013

I wrote my master's thesis on the Philadelphia House of Refuge.

In the 1830s, before mandatory public education, urban elites began the House of Refuge movement to deal with the growing numbers of idle, increasingly Irish working-class and impoverished teens hanging about city streets, more often than not raising the ire of a new and equally growing shopkeeper class. The Houses sprang up in Philadelphia, New York, Boston, Cincinnati, and Baltimore.

Young people were institutionalized by the tens of thousands to mandated terms in these institutions—known by the early twentieth century as reform schools—either by local courts (the typical charge was vagrancy) or by parents who were told that in the Houses of Refuge, their children would be well fed, clothed, and educated. Poor parents, far too often unable to care for their children adequately, at first supported the idea. Soon, though, they learned that the incarcerations—most often not the result of a trial but of a constable's or judge's signature—meant that they would not see their children for years. At least, some believed, their children would be cared for, taught reading, writing, and numbers, and made ready for adult work.

They were wrong.

Their children were warehoused and put to work. Very little formal education was offered. The Houses of Refuge used the children as unpaid labor for all manner of menial work: wood chopping, nail making, baking, horseshoeing, farming. When boys reached 18, thousands were consigned to whaling ships, with or without their parents' consent. Many, of course, would never see home again. All of this was done with the imprimatur of law and in the name of giving poor youth a refuge from their impoverished (and allegedly immoral) homes.

An awful irony was that many of the same elite families that founded the Philadelphia House of Refuge became Philadelphia's earliest public school board members. Moreover, the original Philadelphia public school curriculum was largely lifted from the city's House of Refuge, including manual labor; the public schools were simply the next iteration of civic management of poor children.

Over time, of course, and particularly when public schooling became mandatory in the 1880s, the curriculum branched out. And, needless to say, from the early 1800s, Philadelphia's wealthy sons attended its real schools, the region's private schools.

I was put in mind of my old research when I read of Irish Prime Minister Enda Kenny's long-overdue formal apology in February 2013 to the descendants—and the few still alive—of the thousands of impoverished Irish girls and women who were remanded to what were known as the Magdalene Laundries. The Laundries, begun roughly at the time the Houses of Refuge were founded in America, were places where the poorest of Ireland's girls and women worked for virtually no money, where they were routinely physically and verbally abused by the Sisters of Mercy (how's that for blackly ironic?), where food was scarce, where dormitory heat was almost nonexistent in winter, and where their clothes were allowed to fray to tatters before they were issued new ones.

Patrick Corrigan, the Northern Ireland Programme Director for Amnesty International, wrote in a February 2013 *Huffington Post* blog[6]:

> "Today, it is our generation's and our governments' reputation for honour, not that of the Magdalene women, which is at stake."

Corrigan went on to note some of the highlights of a recent Irish government report on the inmates of ten Magdalene Laundries in the Republic of Ireland:

- Some 14,607 inmates were recorded across the ten institutions.
- Some 1,500 were locked up for more than a decade.
- The average age of inmates was 23; the youngest entrant just nine, the oldest, 89.
- Over a quarter of the Magdalene inmates were ordered there by the state—by the courts, the police, or social services—and almost 40% by priests or other Church bodies.
- Unmarried mothers and girls from broken homes were dispatched to lives of servitude.

That Enda Kenny has issued now a formal state apology is important, however late. It will lead to renewed interest in the history of the Magdalene Laundries and in *The Magdalene Sisters*, a 2002 film, written and directed by Peter Mullan, about four young women given into the custody of the Laundries.

As far as I know, no film is planned about the abuses suffered by America's nineteenth-century urban children—also mostly poor and Irish—in the Houses of Refuge, our proto-public schools. And, of course, there has been no apology.

---

[6] Patrick Corrigan, "Magdalene Laundries: Northern Ireland's Hidden Shame," *Huffington Post,* February 19, 2013.

For Sallie, Long Gone: American Communists, Progressives, and Who Gets to Criticize Our Culture

1980 - 2012

In the summer of 1980, I wrote a book, *Survival & Renewal,* for the World Fellowship Foundation in Conway, New Hampshire, in celebration of the leftist summer retreat's fiftieth anniversary.

I'd been a guest there before, enjoying a wide variety of programs—political, cultural, artistic, economic—involving presenters from all over the United States and overseas. At any one time, as many as 150 guests attended World Fellowship, a stimulating, vibrant place whose activities went beyond lectures and discussions. The rustic setting afforded boating and canoeing and swimming in magnificent Loon Lake; you could hike, play ball, make a clay pot or three, play pick-up basketball and, most of all, just talk a summer away with bright, well-informed people, both adults and kids.

I enjoyed writing the history of the golden anniversary summer session immensely, and I loved meeting people, particularly older people, who challenged me to my core. There were many. I was twenty-nine and barely conscious of the gay rights movement, and what I knew before that summer of women's issues paled when I looked back on those warm months later on that fall. The learning moments in Conway were always rich and often surprising.

And my most intimate learning moment that summer was shocking.

43

Late one August morning, under a gigantic birch tree, I'd just finished reading from *Animal Farm* to a group of young people. As these readings were always open, any adult could pull up a weather-beaten Adirondack chair to listen in as the kids sat on the soft grass. When we finished, the kids left the shade of the birch.

An older woman, Sallie, didn't leave. I remember Sallie's strong blue eyes, her intelligent smile, her long white hair, her green-and-white World Fellowship tee, her black jeans. Then in her late eighties and well known for her outspokenness even among the outspoken, she was a former suffragette, a veteran of old socialist and communist labor movements, and someone who'd put herself on the line more than a few times prior to the Depression, during the civil rights movement, and beyond. She'd known beatings and jail cells and was proud of it, and she was rightly admired.

Sallie had listened intently to my *Animal Farm* reading and my brief Q&A with the children. As I stood to leave, I smiled at her and was walking away when she grabbed my arm hard and yanked me toward her.

"You must never criticize Russia," she admonished me.

"What?"

"You must never, ever criticize the Soviet Union, Jonathan. Ever."

"Sallie. First, I believe I may criticize any nation, my own, or another, when I think it's appropriate. And I was reading *Animal Farm*, Sallie."

"Oh, oh! That's what you say, Mister Suburban Liberal! Mr. Orwell...that bum! He knew he was criticizing the Soviet Union in that trash he wrote, and now these children here will believe that garbage, too!"

"Sallie, I...."

"Jonathan! You must never criticize Russia."

She released my arm, and, later that night, when I sat next to her at a long table for dinner and at a professor's slide lecture, she was as jovial as ever. Perhaps she'd let go of the morning as she'd let go of my arm. More likely, I think, she just assumed I'd taken her teaching to heart.

But I never did.

It still surprises me that a slice of the American Progressive movement finds it easy, if not obligatory, to criticize, loudly and continually, the United States for all its sins (and there are, have been, and will be many American sins), while ignoring those positive things we have done and do. As if, for example, celebrating the Bill of Rights as exceptional and working hard for its proper application is at best sappy and at worst a cover for our collective crimes.

Many American progressives are firmly in Sallie's camp—not nostalgic for Stalin, of course, but clear about what Progressives should and shouldn't criticize. Many suggest we should never criticize other nations or their (left-leaning) political movements because America is huge and powerful and congenitally guilty, and that denies us the right to lodge thoughtful criticism elsewhere.

To those who believe that, I pose these questions. Is it untoward for an American Progressive to criticize:

- the Soviet-style communism that has transformed the northern half of the Korean Peninsula into a massive starvation camp overseen by a military clique?
- South American dictators?
- Al Queda's desire to see your kids dead?
- the flat-footed Israeli action against the flotilla?

- the rich Muslim nations' contempt for and consistent economic neglect of their poor coreligionists in the Near East and North Africa?
- apartheid in South Africa?
- the Soviet practice of not allowing Jews out of the country in any serious numbers until the Gorbachev era?
- Mexican government collaboration with cocaine cartels?
- when African freedom fighters such as Mobutu become president of countries like Zaire and turn a nation into a dictatorship?
- when China imprisons its newest Nobel Peace Laureate or when it murders 3,000 at Tian-an-men Square in Peking in June 1989?

These ten instances alone—each of them an opportunity to assess, to criticize, and to act—tell me that if I am living up to what is best in America, that if I am proudly Progressive, I must not shy away from noting injustices and doing what I can to ameliorate them, no matter where the wrong is, here or overseas.

I love you, Sallie. I honor who you were and the good for which you fought. I honor and will honor, old friend, what wasn't worst in you, but what was best.

When She Was a Filthy Turn of Phrase: "On the Dole"

1980; 2012

N ow that it's again apparently fair game for the far right and its dark-souled, sock-puppet candidates to praise child labor; smear welfare, social security, Medicaid, Medicare, and food stamps; and sneer as they spit the words as filthy phrases, I'll raise up Tamar.

When we met in the 1980s, in the early days of the Reagan recession, Tamar received food stamps. She had recently graduated from Tyler School of Art at Temple University in Philadelphia with a specialty in fiber arts. She's a remarkable batik artist, and yet you may be surprised to learn that there was, at that time, no glut of corporate batik positions, either in Philadelphia, where we met, or in her native New York.

At that time, she was not yet an award-winning social worker.

At first, she was able to find only part-time work, as assistant activities director at the Philadelphia-Germantown YMCA, an age-old, respected community institution in a richly diverse Philadelphia neighborhood. In her years there, she more than tripled activities group membership and began and oversaw dozens of classes, including a variety of low-cost and terrific art offerings.

Eventually—while continuing on with her art, mounting shows, and selling to an increasing number of private collectors—she began to find fulltime posts in social work. She is the very best I've known, and, here in Maryland, she's won formal, statewide recognition for her dedication and excellence.

I'm put in mind of Tamar's use of food stamps not only because of the racially tinged far right rhetoric about those whom Jeremiah, Jesus, and Isaiah demanded we care for rather than demonize, but because superstores such as Costco are now years into accepting food stamps.

Here's the reason: Nearly *half* of our nation's children will receive food stamps at some point during childhood, according to a November 2009 article in the *Archives of Pediatrics & Adolescent Medicine*.[1] Costco and its competition know food stamps are good business.

Now, lest you think this is largely about welfare, know that only 12% of our children are in welfare-receiving families or in families that ever received welfare or in families that will likely ever receive welfare.[2]

And yet half of all American children will, at some point, receive food stamps.

• • •

In the fight against poverty, it's possible—despite demagogues, recession, despite class and race bigotry—to make a difference, to act, to matter. We may, one day, have the guts to fight poverty consistently, agitate and work, work and work harder, *then win*.

---

[1] Mark R. Rank and Thomas A. Hirschl, "Estimating the Risk of Food Stamp Use and Impoverishment During Childhood," *Archives of Pediatrics & Adolescent Medicine,* November 2, 2009.
[2] National Center for Children in Poverty, http://www.nccp.org/topics/welfare.html

Among the ideas that simply must be overcome is the false, small-minded, and largely racist assumption that there's anything close to a one-to-one ratio between food stamps and welfare recipients.

A second and quite insane idea that must go is the suggestion that poverty is impenetrable and intractable because recipients are content, if not wildly in love with, their lot.

And the third idea that we must leave behind is the belief that most food stamp recipients are racial minorities. In fact, if you look up racial, ethnic, and geographic welfare and food stamp distributions rates over the past forty years, you'll find that fully 60 percent of current food stamp recipients are white.[3]

If there is one truth about us, it's that nothing gets done when we hold out for the "right conditions"—when we're waiting to feel better *before* we do good. The reality, as some psychologists have told us for decades, is that we feel better *when* we do good.

The truth is, too, that the ambivalence and outsized self-righteous anger among some progressives in the face of a center-left president is little more than a myopic invitation to power to those who have already told us they'd harm our children with glib indifference.

And the children of poverty? They're *our* children, all of them, who may grow up to be, as Tamar is, world-class professionals who daily give back to the culture that helped them briefly long before.

She and I ask that you reject the lies about a near-majority of Americans, the lies about those who have at one time needed a hand, the lies you may be hearing now from cynical politicians.

---

[3] An interactive map of Supplemental Nutrition Assistance Program demographics is available on the USDA website: http://www.ers.usda.gov/data-products/supplemental-nutrition-assistance-program-(snap)-data-system/go-to-the-map.aspx#.UXieZyt34Oo

Vote when the time comes. But do not wait. Join the anti-poverty efforts of our government and of broad-reaching nonprofit community and religious organizations: support local efforts to help the poor, to aid those who are working and still not making it; help them to help their children.

Join us. Please act. Tamar and I believe that you will.

Blindsided: Confronted By a Former Student After 30 Years 1981 - 2010

(Originally published in *Talking Writing*)

I'm lucky Buddy Clayman walked back into my life two years ago. Few of us get jolted awake by working on a film with a long-lost mentally ill student.

Such luck makes a painful hash of memory, however.

Between 1973 and 1979, Bud Clayman was my student at Akiba Hebrew Academy in Merion, Pennsylvania. While Akiba was no alternative school, students and many of their parents called me "Jon." It felt more than comfortable; it felt right. Other faculty members also had affectionate nicknames, but I was young and insanely naïve enough to believe that my work put me at the humming center of the 1970s *zeitgeist*.

In my twenties and early thirties, I thought I was as successful a teacher as you'd find back then. I was energetic, even dynamic, and, by turns, appropriately serious, comic, intimate. Oh, what I could do with literature and history, with philosophy, comparative cultures, religion, composition. For my students, I was *the* go-to advisor and confidante.

I thought my lack of formal psychological training didn't matter. This was the era of the gut, when many schools, particularly schools run by and for the upper middle and upper classes, expected teacher-advisors to "just know how."

51

Am I making excuses—still? Perhaps. The fact is, I thoroughly missed the signs of Buddy's descent into full-blown mental illness. And by then, he was no longer simply my student; he'd been living with me in my own home.

And I missed it.

• • •

Buddy rented a room in my house in 1981. It had been several years since my first wife moved out, and I was again single; we'd had no children. I'd had no other renters before, but I made the offer to Buddy because he told me living with his family had become untenable. He stayed for about a year.

At first, our time as housemates mirrored the way we'd interacted as teacher and student. Buddy, always a very private guy, would emerge from long periods of solitude in his room to discuss his passions: film, television, and sports.

We often reminisced about Akiba. As a senior, Buddy had written and directed a Jerry Lewis-style faux "telethon" to save Jewish American Princesses from their entitled selves. I'd even provided the inane commercial breaks for what he called "The Buddy Clayman JAP-a-Thon."

Looking back, it may seem in bad taste. But Buddy's writing and Jerry Lewis imitation were brilliant. His two-hour show, presented in an upper middle-class Hebrew high school, had been meticulously scripted with "guests," "pitchmen and pitchwomen," the "afflicted," "the cured," and "corporate donors." Even the rabbis in attendance, who would never have permitted such a thing if they'd known about it in advance, were rolling.

It was a high point for Buddy at Akiba, and he reenacted scenes when we lived together. But as time went on, he did this less often. I assumed he had just grown tired of it.

Buddy never quite understood why I didn't "get" hockey. I'd pretend I didn't know what the sport was:

"No, really? We have a hockey club?"

"They won the Stanley Cup in '80!" Buddy would exclaim.

"The what?"

"Jon!"

Increasingly, after exchanges like this, he'd leave the living room, withdrawing. Still, I thought his consternation was playful. I never sensed his frustration.

Within six months, there were long stretches when he'd punctuate his days and nights by coming quickly downstairs to make a simple sandwich and then return to his room. I do recall trying to engage Buddy in brief conversation; often he would barely acknowledge me. I don't remember questioning him in any depth about all the time he spent alone.

Of course, I should have. Yet, he was in his early twenties by then—an adult, or so I told myself.

He left abruptly. Buddy was badly hurt by something I'd said, although I didn't know that at the time. Within days, he'd shut down.

I didn't see him again for thirty years.

• • •

It's ironic that when I called Buddy in the spring of 2009, it turns out he'd been planning to look me up, too. I had begun doing that, attempting to get in touch with old friends: high school classmates and fellow British teacher-writers we'd lived with when my second wife, Tamar, and I taught in China in the mid-1980s. I was inching toward sixty, a time of reckoning. I was anticipating my fortieth high school reunion in the fall of 2009.

Buddy recognized my voice immediately. He greeted me enthusiastically, saying that he was shooting a film about his combined obsessive compulsive disorder, depression, and Asperger's syndrome. He invited me to Philadelphia to work on a scene in the documentary, and I was happy to oblige.

On the muggy July afternoon that I met Buddy in front of my old house in northwest Philadelphia, I little expected to be slapped in the face at the jump: Buddy looked straight toward the camera, then at me, and announced I'd betrayed him thirty years before.

As Buddy describes it, after days in his room at my house, he emerged late one evening from the second floor. On the stairs, he appeared in a striped bathrobe. I told him he looked like a Holocaust victim.

This is how I remember it: His robe had been wrinkled and dingy. I told him it looked like "standard death camp issue," missing the moment with a bad joke. He'd gone very pale, but he often did. At the time, he said nothing; he ingested my remark silently.

Now I sat there on the stone wall in front of a house I hadn't lived in for years, his former teacher and mentor, flooded with nausea, reminding myself every second that I was being filmed, grabbing my stomach, twisting my shaking, guilty hands.

I admitted that I had no idea I'd hurt him as I did. Even when confronted by a much older Buddy, it took me some moments to remember the incident. The remark had just seemed like more of the banter I thought was intrinsic to our getting on together.

But *why* hadn't I understood? Why hadn't I said more when I could have, asking after him in ways that might have mattered?

Sitting there on the stone wall it hit me hard: Without the safety and cushion the school setting provided us both, the *zeitgeist* I held so dear had been hollow at the core. I'd missed *him*. I'd missed who Buddy was becoming. I'd missed who he was.

Pinned on the wall, I didn't read Buddy's ambush as revenge. I knew I had blindsided myself. I even recall thinking, "He's a film director. He has to make this raw."

And within an hour of the shoot, we were laughing over dinner. He also gave me, on camera, a book of the complete short stories of Joseph Conrad. Buddy told me how much he'd loved the way I taught "H of D."

The fat hardback was wrapped in aluminum foil. I took the book and said with a smile, "No one has given me such a huge brick of marijuana before. Now, you mustn't cut that!"

Buddy laughed, as did the crew. That scene didn't make it into the film.

• • •

While Buddy and I have built on our friendship over the past eighteen months, going to the premiere of *OC87* at the University of Pennsylvania's International House in September 2010 didn't bring me unalloyed joy.

I found myself in the darkened theater (and then well after the lights came up), sitting alone among 300 people, sweating, as if I were waiting for a blade to slice into the back of my neck. Ashamed, I realized I'd been anticipating this for months.

The confrontation scene is brilliantly edited. The film cuts swiftly from the confrontation to Buddy's therapist, who explains to him that Buddy, through the prism of his Asperger's, misinterpreted the remark I had so casually lobbed at him. But what struck me was how callous I'd been as a young teacher. I was the *zeitgeist* of nothing.

In my experience, there are two distinct kinds of oddball teens— those embraced by peers despite their oddities and those who are ignored or even shunned. Because of his incredible humor, talent, and decency, Buddy's peers at Akiba regarded him as odd but "theirs." They embraced him whether or not he fully felt this as a teenager. I know a number of his former classmates have seen *OC87* and responded positively.

That's not an excuse for me missing his illness decades ago. But I didn't worry about Buddy the way I would have about a student ill-treated by others.

Part of the '70s *zeitgeist* also involved a transformation in what it meant to be a teacher and mentor. At the time, we believed in breaking down the old-fashioned power dynamic between teacher and student. At the time, it did feel revolutionary.

Yet, I'm not sure if it ever was. As a writer, I now feel an increased, almost panicky obligation to my subjects, topics, and audiences. These days, before I write, while I write, and as I edit, I live as best I can their moments—not mine.

_____

Note: For more information about the film and current screenings, visit http://oc87.com/home

An Origin, in Shame, of My LGBT Rights Advocacy

1981 - 2012

Well over thirty years back, in the time before we were married, Tamar introduced me to two gay women. Then in their early fifties, Patty and Rachel were longtime, very close friends of her parents, women with whom she'd grown up. Tamar adored them, and, while we haven't had occasion to see them in many years, she loves them still, and rightly.

They're wonderful people. One is a painter who has shown her work often and widely. The other is a novelist who, at times, has been fairly widely read. At the time, Patty had short-cropped, black-and-silver hair. She was long-waisted with narrow, often winking, often arching, eyes and a fun "gotcha!" grin. Rachel was quite round, with a spherical head set atop a large, globelike body. Her very long, thick black hair dropped to the middle of her back. Her serious, onyx eyes hid the existence and sudden power of her often hilariously randy language and social humor. Patty was more reserved. In those days, they were living in a rented house overhanging the crag of a Boston North Shore seaside village.

Tamar and I, visiting friends in Cambridge, drove up one morning to Patty and Rachel's place on the sea rocks. We had coffee, talked and laughed, then strolled through their quaint town.

As we were leaving, Rachel suggested we all go to lunch back in Cambridge. They hadn't been there in a month or more, she said, adding how much they both loved Harvard Square's shops and particularly an exotic popcorn emporium. Patty said she loved the place because the flavors were "part of the popcorn itself," unlike so many imitators whose popped kernels tasted as if the flavors had been "layered on." This popcorn, she said, "had integrity."

As it turned out, that day, I did not.

We visited that shop, bought some popcorn, had burgers, and Tamar said, "Let's stop in on your dad early." She and I were expected for dinner at his Cambridge home in the evening. It sounded good to me, and we drove up from the Square to Dad's house.

What I did then to these two good, talented women was not only inexcusable but was as much of a complete shock to me as it was to Tamar and to them. This was a moment of simple, brutal, personal failure.

As we pulled up to Dad's tree-shaded Victorian, I heard myself say, from a place in me I hadn't previously known, "Tamar and I will step in, say 'hi' to Dad, and be out shortly."

I got out. To her credit, Tamar did not.

I left them all in the car as if they were children, or worse. I went inside and chatted with Dad for several minutes, assuming, wrongly, that the prejudice I'd just found inside myself would naturally have been in—emerged from—him. I felt sure, had we all gone inside, that he'd later ask me questions I'd find uncomfortable. I know now—and I remain surprised that I didn't know then—that he would not have. This was wholly me.

I returned to the car now fully aware of what had surfaced in me. I felt ill. I'd sickened myself. Tamar didn't look at me as we drove Patty and Rachel home, nor on the hour's ride back to Cambridge and, later on, back to my father's. Remarkably, as dismissed and hurt as Patty and Rachel had to have felt, they said nothing about it. They had dignity. That day, I had none. As the two of them and Tamar talked animatedly, I remained mute until goodbyes up on the North Shore.

I have begun and ditched letters of remorse, over and over again. Nothing I have written to them has seemed to me by any measure adequate. Even now, I haven't yet rung them up, after thirty-plus years and numerous articles and public addresses on the rightness, on the simple decency, on the absolute necessity of thoroughgoing equal rights for LGBT citizens. Every time I have published or spoken on the subject, I know that I am conveying what's best in me, what I had always simply assumed was there and just was not on that day.

This hole, this remorse, remains. To make real what I know now, I must do far more than write about equal rights. I must do something that is, ironically, both simpler and more difficult than writing. It may well be that Patty and Rachel couldn't care less, at this distance, about what I did. Yet I now need to make the political quite personal and apologize to these good women for my ancient dismissiveness—and, if it's possible, do so face-to-face.

People's Hero

1986 - 1987 - 2013

When my wife Tamar and I were expelled from The People's Republic of China in May 1986, I was told by many that I must not, for the sake of our Chinese friends, write about that series of events and our other China experiences under my own name. I chose to write this piece—and later pieces for the overseas Chinese student democracy magazine *China Spring*—under the name of the great early twentieth-century American labor organizer Joe Hill.

The woman I tell about here has been in Germany for 23 years and is a German citizen. No harm can visit her with the article's republication. All names in the piece are pseudonyms. The Chinese city I named as the one where I taught is not where I taught.

This piece is my first published essay, appearing in *East-West Magazine* in 1987. That magazine was published from the mid-1940s through the early 1990s, then died. After not having had my copy for 26 years (as a result of far too many moves), I finally located it with the help of a University of Hawaii archivist.

Most remarkably, and after many years of searching, I found the woman I here call Liu Ping. She is now an administrator in a design institute in Berlin. She and her husband have two grown children. In late April 2013, I wrote to what I knew had to be, for various reasons, her email address. She called here almost immediately. We've renewed our friendship.

I've no words to express how grateful I am.

• • •

Liu Ping and I are staring up at ornate red calligraphy from the base of a giant four-sided obelisk, a bumpy thirty-minute ride northwest of Beijing, not far from the Ming Dynasty Tombs. It's a particularly warm and humid day for early spring, and all morning Liu has been going on about the privileged position of artists and designers in China.

"We don't have to care about the political question," she tells me and everyone in earshot, "because we are too special, and of course we know more about life and how the people feel than the party comrades who only know how to tell a person to do something."

I'm a less-than-enthusiastic partner in this mainly one-way ramble; already our conversation, only partly in English, has drawn more attention than the obelisk.

"Liu, please. Let's continue this back in Beijing. There are many people here."

"Joe, I understand. You are nervous and you are ridiculous. I can say what is in my mind. Look up at the writing on the monument. Can you read it?"

I can read only a little of the magnificent blood-red characters and Liu knows it, but I begin to hesitantly translate in fervent hope of taking our dialogue in a new direction. I don't get far.

"How long did you study Chinese? Not enough! Listen: On each side of the monument is a saying from a famous leader. Liu Shao-qi, Zhu De, Zhou En-lai. And, of course, Chairman Mao." She then translates each revolutionary slogan. "You want to know what Chairman Mao says?"

Before I can answer, Liu doubles over, her face convulsed with laughter. She can barely get the words out, and a crowd has

61

assembled to see why the foreigner is making the young Chinese woman shriek so hilariously.

"Chairman Mao says, 'When the People are united they are as powerful as a stallion....' This is too much!" Liu is laughing so hard that the crowd needs no translation now to gather what's been going on and recedes rapidly, wanting no part of this scene.

When we board the bus to continue our pilgrimage to the Great Wall, we have the entire back of the bus to ourselves. Liu affects not to notice the strategic withdrawal and chats on about artists she knows who have narrowly escaped political criticism, recent mindless television editorials, and other topics that leave me, an American who teaches at the university where she used to work, singularly uncomfortable.

Although Liu Ping irked me often while I was in Beijing, aggravating the political anxiety I shared with nearly every other long-term foreigner in China, she soon began to seem to me a new breed of Chinese heroine, an individual with the courage and determination to use the unwieldy, top-down system to her advantage. Her very iconoclasm seemed to endear her to her colleagues, as with a combination of humorous disdain and savvy manipulation, she achieved the goal of nearly every Chinese career woman: a home, a family, and a challenging job in the city of her choice.

When I first met Liu, she was a first-year teacher in the acclaimed architecture department of the university in Nanjing where I went to teach English. Her colleagues and students adored her. On four separate occasions, I was taken, after my own morning lecture, to Liu's office and shown her sketches and paintings. Twice I was taken by one of her students to Lui's painting class so I could "see a perfect art teacher teach." In this way, we got to know each another.

Far from shying away from this unusual public flattery, Liu basked in it: "Yes; it's true. My students love me because I am kind to them and because I hope to teach them very well." In her first year, Liu was singled out by the university as a "model teacher," her name forever to be listed in the Model Teacher archives of the Chinese Ministry of Education. Most recipients modestly file such an award away, but I wasn't surprised when I first visited Liu's flat to see hers prominently displayed on the wall above her small Japanese television.

After that first visit, I stopped by Liu's apartment—a one-room concrete rectangle with a bare bulb in the center of the ceiling—many times. Within its 600 square feet, it combined the styles of New China Austere and Very New Liu décor. Its centerpiece was a sparkling new, green Yugoslav refrigerator, upon which rested a new Crockpot/rice cooker. A set of new black enamel-trimmed pine bookcases incongruously anchored a net of clotheslines that spider webbed up to the low ceiling. The room also contained a half-dozen exquisite cloisonné vases, a set of porcelain teacups, and a collection of model airplanes atop ceramic stands. All of these nice things were gifts that her husband, Zhao, a noted industrial designer and leading figure in his academic department, received for his consulting work.

When I came by one day, he was once again away, consulting with factory managers and public officials in distant cities.

When he returns, Liu tells me as she serves a dinner of scrambled eggs with tomato, rice, and pork-filled dumplings, he will bring more gifts. But there is a more momentous event in the offing: "Joe, in another month, maybe two, my husband and I will move to a new, large apartment in a building for parents. When my baby comes, we will have our new home. When my husband returns from his business, he will discuss this matter with the university leaders."

I ask her a question that's been on my mind. "Liu, several of my women students tell me you are a hero. Why is that?"

She looks proudly about her small room, at the refrigerator, the bookcases, the cloisonné vases, the model airplanes, the Japanese television set, and begins her remarkable story.

63

"You know, I plan all this, but even I did not ever think I could have all this so quickly and, in a little time, a baby and a new home with three rooms. You know, I am only 23 years. My mother and father love to come to my home to see my things. My husband is well known and people give him respect. I have a good job, better than before at your college because here I can live with my husband, and my work is also very interesting. Look."

She stands up and opens one of the bookcase cabinets, removing four large red plastic photo albums. I'd seen one of them. Included are family snapshots and, toward the end, some pictures of us together: Liu, Zhao, and me. The second is jammed with business cards, Chinese, English, Japanese, perhaps 150 in all. The other albums are filled with photographs of designs, models, all kinds of architectural drawings, each photo neatly trimmed behind a plastic guard.

"Joe, there are not many women who can show you books like mine and my husband's. I am very lucky." Liu is speaking softly. "When I worked in the architecture department in Nanjing, before I come to Beijing to join my husband, we are married three years and yet I see him only one time every month, and if I am busy or he is busy, maybe one time in six weeks. And then, at that time, if I see him, maybe I am feeling still alone although I am with him, and maybe I feel angry, and I think maybe he is angry at me because I am so much away from him. Many, many times we are angry with each other, and once I tell my roommate that I think maybe sometime I will have to divorce with my husband. When he leaves to go back to Beijing, I cry all night and say many bad things about him, but really it is that we are alone for each other."

I recalled that an acquaintance at my university who lived in the same building as Liu told me on several occasions about the fights Liu and Zhao had when he came down to stay for a weekend. They would argue, and Liu could be heard crying well past midnight almost every night Zhao was there.

"I know you wanted to live with Zhao," I said reassuringly. "He wanted to live with you, too, of course."

"Yes, but it is not simple. When I graduated from Beijing Central Fine Arts Institute, I hope I will be told I can teach here, but I was sent to your university in Nanjing. My husband asked his leader to help us, but his leader could do nothing. She told him that we must not complain because when she was young woman, she lived in Beijing and her husband lived in Hunan Province, much further than Nanjing, and that her husband joined her after a long time, maybe seven years. She said she saw her husband two times in one year maybe, and she said she was a very sad young woman and that my husband should be happy. Well, we were not happy.

"I decided I would go to Beijing and get a new job. I don't care anymore that so many young women from university never live with their husband for a long time. For me, it is almost three years and it is enough. I began to ask my department leader if I could change my job so I can be with my husband, and for many months he did not have time to listen to me. My husband was very happy that I began to do this, and he told me that if I took my best work and carried it to Beijing, he will try to make an appointment for me with leaders at schools and government offices. My husband knows many people.

"Many months I continue to teach in my department, and my husband has friends in some schools and offices who say they will see me. I travel here to Beijing many times and show my work to many leaders. At the last, two of them tell me that if my department leader says I can go, they will welcome me to work in Beijing! One gave a letter to say that they will welcome me, and I then brought the letter to my architecture department."

"When did you first discuss this with the department chairman—after you were invited to work here?"

"I discuss this with him, I try to, very quickly, of course. But I told you, Joe, he did not want to discuss this thing with me even I show him the letter. So, after long time, I get very angry and my husband

65

is angry, too, because he says I can try harder to discuss my future with my leader. My husband gave me a very angry letter, and he said if I care about my family, I will not care about my department, and I think he is right. So I did a very terrible thing."

Liu's voice lowers. "On the morning after I receive my husband's letter, I taught two classes and then it is time for my lunch. But instead of going to the dining hall with my students, I go to my leader's office. It is only him in there, and he asks what is my question. I tell him that he knows my question and he must help me. He looks at me for long time, and I cannot believe I have talked to him in this way. I try not to have my voice sound so angry, but I keep thinking of my husband's letters and that he says I can be strong for my family. My department leader looked outside the window and I think that he will not speak to me, so then I do something even more terrible."

"What did you do?"

"I hit my fist down on his worktable near his desk, and he jumped up because he was looking outside. Now I am very afraid. He looked away from the outside and at me. He told me, 'You are a very impolite woman. I will have my lunch now,' and he begins to walk from his office. But I stand in front of him and I say, 'Professor Chen! Please listen to me! You *must* help me and my husband and our baby! Professor Chen! Comrade Party Secretary Hu Yao-bang says a husband and wife should try to be together!' Professor Chen is very surprise. Maybe no girl has ever talk to him like this. Then I see he is looking past where I am standing and that he is not looking well because his office door is open and there are some students and teachers gather there because they heard my voice. I think I was not quiet.

"Professor Chen closed the door and told me to sit down and he walked quickly to his desk. He looked inside his desk for a long time and did not look at me. I am very afraid now, Joe, because I do not know what he will do. Of course, Professor Chen is also a Party leader a long time. I feel very hot and my face felt red and I have a big pain in my stomach, but I do not move. I try to look at Professor Chen.

"Then Professor Chen took from his desk a pen and university writing paper. He asks me what do I think: He will write a letter to China Travel Service and suggest that for next three months I work for his department and then after three months, I go to Beijing and work for Travel Service. If Travel Service likes my designs for them, I can stay with them three months and then come back to his department and continue in this way. He asked me what is my idea.

"I tell him thank you but if he can find someone to teach my students, maybe I can stay in Beijing with my husband. He said he will try. Then he walked to the door and locked it, and I worry again. But he smiled at me when he sat down, and he said I was a very impolite young woman and that I must learn to give him more respect. Professor Chen said to me, 'Teacher Liu, I am not so old. When I began to teach, my wife was in Harbin, very far north. We saw each other very little for more than six years until she came here. Then, after three years she was ill and she died. I am not so old, but I still have no wife. I can try to help you and your husband.'

"Now my household is here, Joe, in Beijing, and my husband and I will have our baby and he will be Beijing Citizen and he will go to the children's school at my husband's college and later to the middle school and my husband's college and he will have a good life."

Liu washes the dishes in a communal sink in the dark hall outside her door. She carefully sets the candlesticks and the placemats inside a bookcase. She sweeps the floor under the table. She says, "When we move to our new home, I will buy a machine to clean my floor. I am saving money now for this."

We talk together for perhaps another hour. Liu is tired, and I've become somewhat light-headed with the dinner wine. "I will walk with you to the Guest House and tomorrow I will take you to the train. I am sorry, Joe, that you will leave China before I will have my baby."

• • •

Shortly after Tamar and I left China, I received a letter and a book of sketches from Liu Ping. She related that she and her husband Zhao had recently moved into their new three-room apartment in another part of his campus. Her new design job was going very well. Zhao had been away on consultations twice in recent months; he had brought home a new wooden television stand and a used electric typewriter.

Their son Zhao Ping-xin was born on August 25, 1986. I have his photograph, and no doubt there are a dozen more like it in the Liu-Zhao family album.

Would You Ever Take a Bullet for Someone?

1986 - 1990 - 2011

(First published in *Talking Writing*)

In the spring of 1985, I met Zhang Ying in my Advanced Oral English class at Tianjin University. After our first three-hour session, Zhang, a college junior, stepped up to my desk briskly. Our classroom was in a prerevolutionary building with a pagoda-style roof, seventy miles southeast of Beijing.

Zhang was bold. She asked if she might study with me privately, "to improve my English composition," she said, "for myself, to be better than the rest."

Before I opened my mouth—I was sipping hot tea from a student-provided thermos, as I recall—she assured me that she knew "Americans like money so I can pay you but it will have to be in *renminbi*, not in your dollars, Teacher Wolf-man, because I am only poor Zhang Ying and I have no real money."

I told her I'd accept no payment, that the university was generous with foreign teachers. (Indeed, we earned nearly four hundred times each month what Chinese professors in the English Department at the time did.) With that, our bargain was sealed. Zhang applied herself to one writing assignment after another, for ten weeks that first semester.

During our lessons, I used writing prompts that were designed to spark more than simple answers or a single sentence. In response to

"Would You Parachute from an Airplane?," for example, Zhang wrote:

> "I would not! The only person who would do that who is not a soldier needs to be in a hospital for people who are not very well in their emotion. If my husband did this I would kill him."

I still wonder if learning to write in another language is like taking a leap into space. You could say I was the equivalent of a parachute for an eager student like Zhang, but it turned out I was flimsy silk. In China, I discovered that such a leap could be terrifying, with consequences I doubt she imagined at first.

Then again, maybe Zhang could imagine what would happen and did it anyway. Our lessons continued for the next two terms that I was in the People's Republic of China—until I got myself thrown out.

• • •

In February 1985, Tamar Weiss and I had been married just two years when we arrived at Tianjin University to teach. I had recently completed an eleven-year, just-out-of-grad-school stint of teaching humanities at Akiba Hebrew Academy west of Philadelphia. Tamar had served in several combined social work and art-teaching positions in the Philly area.

Simply put, we wanted new challenges. The idea of teaching overseas appealed to our joint sense of adventure and began as something of a lark.

I was 34. While Tamar had studied art in Siena, Italy, I'd never been abroad. We were both excited by the prospect of immersing ourselves in a world as alien as post-Mao China a decade after the infamous Cultural Revolution.

It came together very fast, even though China was just then reopening to the West. I wrote a brief letter to its Ministry of

Education in September 1984; we had Tianjin University's invitation by early November.

We flew there on Valentine's Day—holding hands and talking nonstop. We didn't study Mandarin before we went. We learned a little once we were there (we were fascinated by all things Chinese, maybe as dizzy about the place as we were with each other), but we remained cocooned in English.

• • •

To Zhang's vociferous consternation, we began with the fundamentals of constructing a paragraph. I was struck by how she and many of my Chinese students, all accomplished in the sciences, thought little of ending almost any kind of paragraph in the middle.

Proper paragraphs, I'd tell Zhang, did readers a favor when their last sentence brought readers back to core ideas in an interesting way.

Zhang's tart response: "You want my writing to look backwards, Teacher Wolf-man. I want to move ahead. We are taught that we must move ahead."

She wasn't the first to complain about the basics of English composition. Early on, I asked another class if they were confused by my approach. Most students agreed that my desire might be bound up in what one called "a Western need" for simplistic closure.

Another scientist-student, in his mid-forties, wondered if I failed to realize that a paragraph is just one small part of a larger whole. I might wish to develop "more patience," he instructed me, to content myself to wait for "an interesting, ultimate ending," much as he and his colleagues summoned patience before drawing conclusions in a series of related experiments.

When I asked if Chinese students in the humanities also saw their writing this way, he reminded me that history was a process, as Marx had taught, and could be approached scientifically. History,

71

Mao had said, like progress in science, was *yi-ding!* Certain! Inevitable!

This student was one of the few who always wore a Mao jacket. He had an angular face, and his hair was closely cropped. I never asked him if he'd been a Red Guard during the Cultural Revolution—that would have been poor form—but it wouldn't have surprised me.

I decided not to turn this into a political discussion I couldn't win. I just told the class that they'd have to humor me if and when I asked for a paragraph.

Was Comrade Scientist serious? The first time I gave another group a test that asked for three-to-five sentence responses to oral questions, those students, to my shock, openly consulted one another for answers.

"You think 'cheating,' I know," Zhang said when I asked her about it. "The tests you give us are not university entrance examinations. We are already here; we have passed the examinations. Here, students succeed together."

While Comrade Scientist might have been toying with me, I know Zhang was not. I also wasn't the only Western teacher on that campus to have experienced such a forehead-slapping moment.

Months later, I asked a Chinese professor in the English Department if she'd ever seen students working together like this. She studied me closely, smiled, then nodded *and* shook her head—before wishing me a good day.

• • •

After we were invited to teach in Tianjin, we learned that it and Philadelphia were Sister Cities. Our Philadelphia Mayor's Office even named Tamar a cultural representative. We lived in Tianjin University's Foreign Experts Guest House with perhaps twenty other English teachers—Brits, Canadians, Aussies, and other Americans—on its sprawling, 30,000-student campus.

Tian-Da (Big Tianjin), the university's informal name, is a leading national science and technology institute that was founded in 1895. By the mid-1980s, its administrators had started inviting Western teachers such as Tamar and I for short stays. The plan was that we'd help prepare professors and students for participation in overseas conferences and research symposia. English had already become the *lingua franca* at such international academic events.

Tamar's batik-design classes at the Thomas Eakins House of the Philadelphia Art Museum had always been small, with no more than ten students. Now she taught at the Tianjin Fine Arts College, one hour from Tian-Da across this heavily trafficked Chinese city of nine million. Her classes contained up to 30 students, yet the self-discipline of the Chinese made them feel smaller.

The Chinese art students were a joyous, talented bunch, and Tamar loved it. She helped connect Tianjin artists with those in our sister city back home. Riding her shiny, black, factory-new Flying Phoenix bike every day, she really did see herself as an ambassador.

Still, the seeming openness of the Chinese to other cultures was both real and an official fantasy. We enjoyed going to overflowing banquets with our hosts, regaling them with tales of "strange" American customs, laughing at our joint misunderstandings. But from our first days there, Tamar and I saw how the African students on campus were regarded.

On the surface, they were housed and fed far better than Tian-Da's Chinese students. While Chinese dorms were continually coated with coal dust in the cold months, the African dorm was kept almost spotless by Chinese workers. The African student cafeteria served a much greater variety of dishes in a far more hygienic setting. They enjoyed fresh vegetables regularly, even fresh fish on occasion. The Chinese student cafeteria diet seemed to serve nothing but pork-filled buns.

73

But although the Africans were treated as honored guests, many Chinese students resented this. The university assigned no workers to clean the Chinese student quarters; the Chinese students were left to fend for themselves. They often complained bitterly about having no time for much at all after study, sleeping, and eating.

They understood the political value of treating the African students well—I knew many who could parrot the right phrases, much as Comrade Scientist knew Mao's lines about the inevitability of history—but that didn't mean they liked it.

Even Zhang, in the midst of quizzing me about a popular American movie at the time (*Kramer vs. Kramer*) suddenly asked, "Why do the blacks smell oddly? Are they dirty?"

I was stunned. While I'd taught no African American students at Akiba Hebrew Academy, a private high school, such overt forms of racism were especially striking to a Philly resident. When I taught for a semester at the Community College of Philadelphia, all my students were black or Hispanic. Tamar, for her part, had worked with many at-risk children and young adults at the art museum in Philadelphia.

• • •

Zhang's first composition assignment struck a raw nerve in her: "Describe Yourself and a Friend. Use Descriptive Adjectives." She wrote maybe eight sentences, noting that her western province's typically round face, rounder-than-usual eyes, dark skin, and long thick black hair with "reddening streakings" made her look "foreign" compared with all the far lighter skinned Han in Eastern China.

In fact, more than 90 percent of Chinese are of Han descent. (For that matter, nearly 20 percent of the world's population is.) And when you're an ethnic minority in China, you're a real minority.

When she'd arrived from Xin-jiang Province two years earlier, Zhang told me, "People said I didn't look Chinese." She'd been teased, a great deal at first, by other university men and women— although they'd stopped when word got around she didn't mind using her fists. According to Zhang, one smartly flattened nose had brought the teasing to a quick halt.

In her composition, she wrote that she stood "a little short than Teacher Wolf-man," which made her about 5'6" in black canvas Chinese slip-ons. Tamar guessed she weighed 130 pounds. To 23-year-old Zhang, that made her "incredible fat; it is why they every day call me behind of my back *bu hau kan* [ugly]."

But her written description of her friend was far more forgiving:

> "Of course, Liu is Han and very pretty. She is small and short than I. Her face is oval-shape. Her hair is black. All of it is black and long. Mine is longer. My hair is less black. The hair of Liu does not extend past her back's middle. Mine does extend."

That's how Zhang's initial rewrite concluded. It gave us our first opportunity to do some sentence combining, and by the final draft, which grew to twelve sentences, she had wrapped up her core ideas well: "Even though in my hometown I am thought of as pretty, Liu is thought of as pretty here. I am not and I feel sad."

• • •

The Tian-Da campus was unlike any in the West and not just because of its architecture. It had no grass. Between 1966 and 1976, during *Wen-ge*, Mao's Great Proletarian Cultural Revolution, Red Guards had ordered students and faculty to pull up all the grass and to shoot the campus birds. Appreciating greenery and sweet bird songs were considered emblems of corrupt, Western bourgeois culture.

75

Even in 1985, close to a decade after the Cultural Revolution's last days, no one had re-sodded our campus. There were newly planted hedges, bushes, and trees, but birds were still scarce.

The barrenness of Tian-Da created a feeling of sensory alienation that Tamar and I never shook off. It was our own Gobi Desert of dust each day it didn't rain. When it did rain, the university turned to mud, often swamping its bike paths and roads. Coal was piled outside nearly every campus building, and coal dust turned the mud a turgid gray.

Given our evident shock at the state of Tian-Da, Zhang and others quietly shared with us the new pieties—a Party line that said Mao himself had the right ideas at the start of the Cultural Revolution but was increasingly undermined by his radical comrades, including his now-disgraced, imprisoned wife.

Then, as now, the University's brochures showed green grass and mature trees, but in the mid-eighties that was pure fiction. Even when we got off campus, the city seemed to be a mass of bricks, construction sites, and new shopping malls. Only when we took trains through the countryside did we see green agricultural fields. Some of Tianjin's parks had begun to show life, but they weren't near campus, and we rarely biked to them.

We saw no lush urban greenery until we traveled back to the States for summer break in 1985. When we picnicked with friends just east of the Schuylkill River, that Philadelphia public park looked like paradise.

• • •

In subsequent weeks, Zhang penned nine other English paragraphs by hand. They were mostly descriptive and on a variety of topics. With each draft, her paragraphs became clearer and better structured, fit for use in longer essays.

I can still hear her excitedly reading her answers aloud before handing them to me for correction. In response to "Would You Ever Give Money to a Beggar?," she wrote:

"I would not! Begging is an illegal activity and it is unnecessary in a Socialist Republic with Chinese Characteristics. In the U.S. they are punished very severely. If a beggar is found in Beijing, he is taken from the street and he is given food and a place to live and clothing. He is given by our government a place to stay for many months. Maybe he will stay years. Begging is like stealing and in China stealing touches the law. If my husband would hear I had done this, even he is studying now at Beijing University, he would be angry."

With "If You Have a Child, Will You Encourage Him/Her to Join the Military?," her response was emphatic:

"Of course I would do that! We owe much to the People's Liberation Army. My child will be a soldier like the soldiers who defeated Jiang Jie-shir [Chiang Kai-Shek]. Gloriously Mao Zedong defeated him even it took many years! Then my son will study in an important university."

Zhang appended a note to this one suggesting I buy up quantities of used, pea-green and navy Chinese Army overcoats for resale to young Americans back in the States. She said that while making a profit in China remained suspect, for a foreigner it would be fine. A 500-percent markup was reasonable, she told me. While Zhang never said so, I got the impression that she wanted to be my partner in this venture.

• • •

Perhaps the Tian-Da campus itself, this dusty ongoing monument to zeal, should have worried us more than it did. Yet, Tamar and I didn't realize for nearly eighteen months after our arrival in China how far zeal could go.

By the spring of 1986, we were scheduled to teach the following fall at Sun Yat-Sen University in Guangzhou (Canton), a three-hour Pearl River motorboat ride north of Hong Kong. I was thrilled. Sun Yat-Sen had a decidedly greener, palm-treed campus than Tian-Da; Hong Kong was already my favorite city.

We never made it.

• • •

China had hosted African graduate students since well before the Cultural Revolution. "Our Little Brothers"—African nations like Burundi and Tanzania that had liberated themselves from the West—sent their best to Chinese technology institutes for graduate study. They usually remained three years, learning written and spoken Chinese the first year, earning doctorates in the next two.

Since the 1960s, Chinese investment in Africa's infrastructure and modernization projects, often run by those same African grad students when they returned home, had been enormous. But one night in May 1986, all the official policies and socialist language couldn't stop a sudden onslaught of racism.

The Chinese Women's National Volleyball Squad, ranked first in the world, was slated to play a long-ballyhooed match against the powerful Cuban women's team. All the Cuban players were black.

Like millions throughout China, our campus had gone crazy for weeks in anticipation of the showdown. Hundreds of male students had written devotionals to team members, many proposing marriage. The team, in fact, had an official letter-reader who fielded and replied to the lovesick.

Then the Chinese lost to the Cubans. It was a non-tournament game, and I don't recall the exact score, but it was definitive—and an unexpected upset.

• • •

Toward the middle of our third semester together, Zhang had completed several essays on topics of her choice, including her desire, one she shared with many Chinese, to one day study in the West.

Throughout our writing sessions, she and I discussed the possible uses of American English idioms like "break the law"—the literal Mandarin uses "touches"—or "taking a bullet" for someone.

But I learned from her, too.

For example, in her rewrite of a paragraph called "Would You Ever Take a Bullet for Someone?," Zhang specifically added that she'd do so for her husband. She told me this was important to understand, because traditional Chinese ideas about family had been severely undermined by the Cultural Revolution, when spouses had denounced one another. She also wrote:

> "For my family only and in battle for a soldier who is in my group, yes, I would do this. I am sorry, teacher. I cannot take a bullet for you. You are not my country and you are not my family. I hope you will understand my thinking."

• • •

The day after the Cubans beat the Chinese team, Tamar and I invited Zhang to join us at the African students' dorm that evening. Those students had planned a cultural exhibition and dance in the dining hall of the dorm to honor the twenty-third anniversary of the Organization for African Unity (now the African Union). The night of May 25, 1986, began with dance performances, art exhibitions, and delicious spicy fish to eat.

We danced among a hundred or so African graduate students and twenty or more Western teachers. About ten Chinese women attended. The dorm event was supposed to wind up at midnight. But at 11 p.m., a riot broke out. Hundreds of Chinese students (including many of my own) attacked us there, hurling bricks, rocks, and bottles, shattering every window of the dining hall.

What had the African students done? What had Zhang and the other Chinese women done? What on earth had *we* done?

We knew, as did Zhang, that some Chinese students assumed she was there to dance with *wai guo-ren* (foreigners) and *hei-gwei* (black devils). Throughout the night, we heard rioters chanting that noxious phrase. The rocks and bricks and bottles kept coming.

Within minutes, we were crouched in the dorm's kitchen and small offices. University officials did nothing but watch. Some old China hands among us Westerners said that, since the Cultural Revolution, collective memory of Red Guard violence was still raw; officials would hesitate a very long time before doing anything to upset mobs of students. Even the city police were skittish. Some of us called them repeatedly only to be dismissed with quick, cheery comments like "You'll work it out!" and fast hang-ups.

It seemed clear that we'd fallen into an unlucky confluence of popular culture and racism. The loss of the Chinese team had challenged the generally held fantasy of Han superiority. The bubble had been pricked by "black devils"— *hei-gwei*—and I promise you, the drumbeat of that chant, the one we heard throughout the night, matched in viciousness any slur ever flung at black students in 1950s Little Rock.

The next day, I recall thinking how ironic it was to have spent much of that evening dreamily swaying to Lionel Richie's "All Night Long," an African student favorite. And then, how we all stood huddled in the rear of the window-shattered dining hall—then later, crouched in back rooms as we protected one another from repeatedly threatened physical attack all night long—well into the next morning.

• • •

The mob demanded that we American and British teachers—*their* teachers—hand over our African hosts. We handed over no one. When the police showed up to restore order at about 7 a.m., the tired mob largely dispersed on its own. University officials now made a show of coming to our rescue, warning us not to discuss what had happened.

The Africans were led out and detained at a yet to be opened hotel on the city's outskirts. Later that day, we brought them magazines, sodas, and candy.

We'd always understood that our phones were tapped, but I still called several African embassies. We were certain the Chinese wouldn't, and if the embassies remained unaware of what had happened, Tian-Da officials would keep the men detained as long as they wanted.

Not long after I made the calls, the police returned the whole group of students to campus. But several of them, probably chosen at random, were forced to make a ludicrous public apology for an attack they did not provoke, in which they did not participate, and for alleged injuries no Chinese student had suffered.

Then there was Zhang. Because she was our friend and had attended the dance, my budding writer was officially labeled: she'd aided foreigners unfriendly to China.

Tamar and I were expelled within days. I'd called the embassies, after all. Chinese officialdom claimed we'd fomented the riot; we were lucky not to have been disappeared. We could have been charged with incitement, and, as we learned later, we nearly were.

While we got out, Zhang Ying remained, a marked woman. Her application several months later for Party membership was laughed off the pile, shutting all the right academic doors. Her stipend would never rise; her husband's career in economics would stall. Urged to divorce her, he hung tough. Zhang was never physically abused, but she endured over forty separate interrogations about her foreign contacts.

"My child will be a soldier like the soldiers who defeated Jiang Jie-shir. Gloriously Mao Zedong defeated him even it took many years! Then my son will study in an important university."

• • •

Once home, now in Grafton, Vermont, Tamar and I were determined to get Zhang out, too. Under a pseudonym, I began to edit the now long-defunct *China Spring*, a democracy movement journal out of New York. Its chief editor, Wang Bingzhang, has since been lost in the vast Chinese penal maze.

We heard nothing of Zhang for three years. Then came June 4, 1989, and the massacre of 3,000 pro-democracy demonstrators at Tiananmen Square.

Later that summer, I received an unsigned letter I knew was from Zhang. I recognized her handwriting, and at that point, she was the only conceivable person in China who'd be writing to me. She'd found me through a relative of mine who taught at a well-known American university. She was desperate to leave, frightened to her core by the ubiquitous purges after Tiananmen.

She noted that she practiced her English composition daily but had no teacher. Still, she felt sure that "my English writing is now good enough to get a U.S. graduate school to accept me."

Zhang enclosed a tightly written English paragraph, championing her claim to become a doctoral candidate in engineering. Her statement required no correction. It wrapped up boldly, neatly capturing her paragraphs' core ideas, calling for her to be accepted on the basis of her academic record, work ethic, and certainty that she'd make lasting professional contributions.

A week later, I received transcripts with an application to the University of Cincinnati and six other engineering programs. I was to forward them with a cover letter of my own. Zhang wrote, "I want Cincinnati because it is the Home of the Reds." In my cover, I noted that her composition skills included ironic humor. She went seven for seven.

Now she needed official permission to study abroad, not a small feat for a person already in bad odor with the authorities. I won't go into detail except to say that Zhang, her husband, and her family scraped; Tamar and I scraped—and people were bribed. (Zhang reminded me later with an enormous grin that bribery, like begging, is illegal in China.)

Money went to university leaders, local police and party officials, others. A long period followed during which we heard nothing.

• • •

In August, 1990, more than three years after we'd left China, Zhang's call came. Her tone was businesslike. This was it: I was to meet her at JFK the next morning. She knew she might never return home.

I drove down from Vermont and slept at a friend's. Her arrival was delayed a day when her plane attempted to lift off, spun, lurched like a drunk, and passed out on the tarmac in Shanghai. The next day, the plane stayed aloft and landed safely.

I won't forget the moment we met again. She looked the same as she had in Tianjin: broad shouldered and healthy, her hair still thick and very long. She wore jeans and a button-down striped top. We stopped two hours up I-91 at a Pizza Hut in Connecticut. Zhang ordered Pepsi and pepperoni. She said the women's room was nicer than her dorm room.

Soon after we drove up the gravel drive at the farmhouse, Tamar and Zhang hugged long and hard. Zhang said, "I'm so thirsty." I turned

83

on the tap and drew deliciously cold water from our well. Zhang, used to drinking only very hot tea because no sane Chinese ever sips untreated ground water, stared at me. I remembered that stare from years before.

"You bring me, poor Zhang Ying, from Tianjin, China, to Vermont, USA, just to kill me?" Then she smiled. She took the glass, swallowed gingerly, and survived.

I Gave My Special Ed Student Elvis and a Rifle

1988 - 2010

Tall, rail thin, and very pale, Gary was nearly twenty and a high school special ed senior when we met in 1988. As hard as he'd tried, Gary hadn't graduated. His disabilities primarily lay in reasoning skills and reading comprehension. These challenges, though, were not why we met. Gary was also showing-to-class challenged.

We met often as his ditching class habit landed Gary at my door and, I suppose, because I took an extra interest in him and in all of our developmentally disabled kids. When I became dean of students at Gary's gorgeously situated public high school in southeastern Vermont, it fast became clear that its board would rather have paid nothing for special programs and that if the feds weren't going to fund them fully, the kids could go hang. Board members never actually said that, but it's what a majority of them meant when they railed against federal mandates, from having to replace ramps to having to hire a useful number of reading specialists for poor readers such as Gary.

So, I did take an interest, often sitting with them at lunch (they were not generally welcome at other tables), running baseball card raffles for them, and coaching a few in public speaking so they could make brief announcements at assemblies. I was, of course, by no means the only adult at the school who cared for these kids. It felt good to do it, though, and the feeling lingers.

When Gary was first sent to my office for cutting class, he quickly noticed the laminated Elvis placemat pinned to my corkboard. He stared at the photo's "signature."

"Mr. W., when'd you get this? My mom *loves* Elvis! No one said you knew The King!"

I told Gary that my brother bought it on a tour of Graceland.

Gary asked, "You mean your whole family knew him, too?"

I tried to clear it up and explained the consequences of further class cutting.

Gary said, "But she's so unfair!"

"Who?"

"Mrs. Trombley flunked me on a test only because she says I got the seasons wrong."

"What?"

"The four seasons, Mr. W. Just the four seasons."

"What did you say they were?"

"Mr. W.! Everyone knows that. You're a flatlander and you'll always be. You ain't from here. The seasons? More'n four anyways. So I didn't know which four to put. Deer. Deer Muzzleloader. Black Bear. Turkey Bow and Arrow. Turkey Shotgun. Moose. That's five. Trombley don't know what's what at all." He shrugged bony shoulders and shook his head.

"*Mrs.* Trombley."

"Yeah. Missis. But she says I flunked because I don't know about spring 'n winter 'n such, and I needed to pass it. I want to get outa high school so I can work for my uncle Mark. He says he won't hire me at the store except I graduate. She says she won't say I'm ready."

I exacted a promise that Gary would attend classes. Then I spoke to Rita Trombley, and we agreed that we could find our way clear to passing Gary on this test, despite his Hunting License Theory about the four seasons. After all, I told her, he showed his knowledge of the more traditional four seasons in my office, and I told her that I bet I could find a special ed kid in northern Jersey in 1966 who'd swear that Frankie Valli was a Season. And that Jersey wouldn't have fallen into the Atlantic. I also suggested that her schedule the following year would have her hour break just before lunch, something I knew she considered a perk, one she'd never had. And the rest of that test? Gary had done enough, barely, to pass.

But Gary showed up at my office not three weeks later, this time brought in by our bus coordinator—burly, bearded Mike—a moment after I'd heard a muffled scream from outside. It was just past 3:30, and Gary had been absent that day. I rose from my chair.

As Mike hauled Gary by the scruff into my office, I noticed the young man was walking stiffly and that he had a long, narrow bulge with a steel tip emerging from his left pant leg. It was a deer rifle. I asked Mike to leave us. Gary leaned, frightened, against my office window.

"Uh, Gary? Why do you have a rifle in your trousers?"

"Ain't loaded, Mr. W."

"I'm pleased. But I'm sure you know that you can't bring guns to campus. Where were you today, anyhow?"

"Huntin'."

"Why'd you come back to school at dismissal, and why in hell did you bring your hunting rifle?"

"Uh. I was out huntin' with my uncles and I needed a ride home and theirs is in the other direction—mine's up the mountain, you know that, you been there...." (I had.) "And so they dropped me and I just got on the bus to go home but I remembered I had this rifle...."

At this point, I told Gary to take the thing from his pants and show me it wasn't loaded and to give me the rifle and any unspent cartridges. He did.

Gary continued. "So they dropped me at the bottom of the driveway. Then when I was gettin' up the hill, up the driveway there...." Gary pointed out my window. "I knew I had to hide my rifle."

"But not very well. Someone saw the muzzle."

"Yeah. That girl screamed. Why'd she yell? It's unloaded." Then: "You gonna spell me?"

"Expel you? And, Gary, she couldn't know it was unloaded."

"I guess."

"This is very serious, Gary. You scared people on a bus. Very foolish decisions to skip school and then to bring your rifle here. They should've driven you home."

Gary looked ill. I excused myself, took the rifle, told Gary to stay put, and walked to my principal's office, having asked my secretary to alert me if she saw Gary leave. After some time, the principal called the superintendent and shared a proposal I'd made a few minutes earlier.

An hour on, Gary, the principal, and I drove up Gary's snow-blown mountain to his family's trailer. We asked Gary to explain the situation to his wheelchair-bound father and to his mom. We all agreed that we wanted Gary to finally graduate and go to work for his uncle. I told Gary's mother and dad that we'd hold on to the rifle, the unspent shells, and Gary's hunting license until graduation, and that, for the balance of the year, he'd do supervised study at lunch whenever a test was scheduled. They thought it was a good deal.

After graduation, we held a very short return-the-rifle-and-ammo ceremony in my office. Gary smiled more broadly than I'd seen most kids smile by that point in my career.

As he and his family turned to leave, I unpinned the "autographed" Elvis Presley placemat from my corkboard.

"Gary," I said, "take Elvis. The King would be happy, I think, for you to have him."

———————————————

Note: Names in this piece have been changed to preserve the privacy of those involved.

Fingers in a Jar

1988 - 2010

A reason I added administration to humanities teaching was to get closer to families, to help children and parents sort out problems and, together, plan futures. On occasion, it meant serving as a catalyst in a family breakup. In one case (and I'm pleased to say only in this case), I was instrumental in separating twin teenage girls from their mom, permanently. Given the circumstances, I'd do it again.

Among the least pleasant and, at the same time, most critical aspects of my work was partnering with state social workers. Often, that was the surest path we could take toward justice for hurt kids. In rural Vermont, I worked with them on a number of cases. The strangest case a social worker and I worked on together started, as many do, as a result of extended truancy.

Our combination middle/high school housed grades 7-12 and served five towns—although that's misleading, since we welcomed children who lived in places unrecognizable as towns. Farmlands and mountainsides may legally be parts of towns, but they don't feel as if they are. Our school took children from one solidly middle-class town, where our school was located, and several outlying ones, up to twenty miles from campus, all distinctly less wealthy.

One of those outlying towns, Cavendish, was economically depressed and had been for some time. The numbers of cars and pickups up on cinder blocks that you'd see from main streets were many, but they were well outnumbered by those that accumulated on decrepit properties off winding secondary asphalt, and then dirt, roads. The roofs and porches of houses and outbuildings were continually in disrepair on many of these roads; plots and yards were continually uneven and overgrown. Sad poverty was always on display, even as the town sent many very fine kids to us every year.

Perhaps a third of our kids came to us from Cavendish, and in the fall of 1988 so did fourteen-year-old Marlee and Donna Rayburn. When they enrolled in our seventh grade, their transcripts were in order. They had attended Cavendish Elementary School for six years. No one at that school had filed a single truancy report. Their official attendance rates were within normal range.

The twins attended our school without incident for three weeks or so, then stopped. By the end of the first week in October, none of my calls to the home had been returned. Subsequent calls to the Cavendish Elementary School resulted in no help, and I got the clear impression from the school nurse that she was well pleased to have been rid of the Rayburn girls and had no interest in discussing them. Same reaction from the principal, although she did tell me that there had been no father in the house for some time. Just how long she couldn't recall. I let the new district superintendent know what was up.

I called Ben Deutsch, a state social worker with whom I'd worked before, and we drove out to the Rayburn home on the second weekend without contact.

By the time we found it, off a tangle of dirt roads, it was dusk, and the beaten old four-story Victorian looked, I have to say, Poe-spooky. Framed by huge windblown maples, its creepiness nearly dissuaded us from stepping from the car. I hesitated at the porch steps but then remembered that Boo Radley's house, though smaller, presented a similar daunting challenge to Atticus Finch's daughter, Scout, and that, in the end, Miss Scout was brave and Boo Radley a harmless, angelic hero.

91

Ben said, "We're here. Let's see who's home."

The house lights were off. We went to the door. Ben pushed a ringer; nothing. My knock opened the door. Nothing but wind. My thoughts leapt crazily from *To Kill A Mockingbird* to, of all things, Moe, Larry, and Curly realizing that they're talking to the Living Dead.

We should have left for home straight away. Instead, I went to the car and got a high-intensity flashlight. As I shone the light into what once had been intended as a living room, we saw clutter, more clutter in one room than I'd ever seen in one space. And dozens and dozens of wax candles in various stages of use.

I called out a hello to no response. I was about to shut the door and turn back to the car when Ben stepped inside. I shone the light for him and followed.

We saw it at once.

On a high mantle above a hearth was a large glass jar with a cork stopper. It was filled with liquid and what looked like a human hand. Intrepid Ben climbed over small tables, garbage, books, dead candles, and supermarket newspaper inserts to reach it. When he brought it down, it was clear that the jar also held fingers—children's and those of small animals.

There was no one at that house, not an adult, not a child. And this was the late eighties; neither Ben nor I had a cell phone. Ben looked at me and said he could legally take the jar. I had no idea if that were true. He placed it in the trunk, and we drove it to Ben's office. He handed over the jar to the authorities next morning. I kept in touch with Ben and the state policewoman who had been assigned to investigate. We all wanted to find those kids.

Two weeks later, she did. Marlee and Donna Rayburn showed to school. They appeared thinner than I'd remembered them but otherwise seemed in reasonably good health, with their fingers intact. They said they'd been in New Hampshire visiting ill relatives.

Truth was, they'd been in Maine, attending what Ben found out later was a series of religious rituals. Their mother, Elaine, told us the following week that she herself would educate her daughters. They'd be trained as priestesses. I didn't even want to know in what religion. Mickey Rourke and Robert De Niro's magnificent and terrifying *Angel Heart* with Charlotte Rampling as a voodoo priestess did horrid dances in my head. That film had already kept me up nights.

A month or so later, social services moved to take Marlee and Donna Rayburn. The hearing was held three months after that, in late January. In the interim, the girls attended school sporadically. They grew thinner and paler each time I saw them. At the hearing, I was asked to describe the girls' attendance record: they had, to date, been truant well over 85 percent of the term. I was asked to say how they appeared to me, physically, as compared to most young teenage girls at our school. I testified that the girls looked increasingly thinner but that I was not an expert on nutrition or malnourishment. I did say I'd worked in schools since the late 1960s and that, to me, these two looked pretty pale and pretty thin in comparison to other girls.

Ben and I described what we found at the house, its general condition and, of course, the jar and its contents. Subsequent social services and police investigations found cultic paraphernalia and some evidence of small animal sacrifice. The mother was indicted, tried, and convicted on a number of counts of animal cruelty. The girls were taken by social services over their and their mother's screams (I was told), and a week or so later were placed with a family up north. Ben later said they were attending school regularly. I was given no further information.

I never learned whose hand, whose fingers, were in the jar, although those twins—and that jar—stay with me.

93

Note: Names in this piece have been changed to preserve the privacy of those involved.

My People: The Wobblies

1990 - 2011

I dreamed I saw Joe Hill last night,
Alive as you or me.
Says I, "But Joe, you're ten years dead."
"I never died," says he.
"I never died," says he.

—Alfred Hayes/Earl Robinson

Though she died in the mid-1990s, I saw my Grandma Sadie last week at my sister's house. She lives on in sepia, over the hearth, as she looked in 1917 in her teenage flapper's garb— grinning broadly, playing her ukulele, resplendent in a grass skirt, hat, and high-laced black boots. I saw her photo in a new light— perhaps because we had laid my dad to rest a few hours earlier—and recalled a night, 22 years past, when she revealed to me more than I'd ever known before about how I come so honestly to my political commitments.

The night before my wife Tamar and I adopted our son Graham in Florida in January, 1990, we took Sadie to a deli. Sadie and my Grandpa Izzy had moved from the Bronx to pre-Mickey Mouse Orlando in 1954, when there were no skyscrapers and few sidewalks. She was originally from Paterson, New Jersey, at the

95

time a cauldron of union/boss/police tension. Sadie and Izzy had stayed in Orlando, opened a mom-pop, retired.

When we flew down for the adoption, Sadie had been living for some time—Izzy having been betrayed by a bad heart in 1966—in a modest yet well-kept building. She insisted that we and our new son stay with her for the week. ("What trouble could it be...and the price of a hotel!?") When she wasn't transfixed by our son, Sadie was

96

devoted to television news and to debating, always from the Left, any issue raised, whether in the lobby of her building or with us.

After she ordered her pastrami on rye and strawberry shake, Sadie leaned across the table. "Jon, now that you have a son, now that you're going to be a father, I want to tell you, both of you, about your family."

Sadie told us some stories I'd already heard—about Izzy's thieving partner in the Manhattan fur trade, their various other business ventures and failures, how manly her Izzy had looked in those quaint, two-piece swimsuits at the New York beaches, details of her family's coming from Eastern Europe, and how she was born in London on the way.

Then she told me something I never knew before: "Your great-grandfather—my father—and his father were Wobblies. Do you know who they were?"

I did know of the Wobblies, the Industrial Workers of the World, and their at times vicious competition with the American Federation of Labor. I knew of their sometimes anarchic vision of a capitalist-free America, their insistence on racial and ethnic union inclusion (an ideal the AFL then spurned), and their conviction that labor organizing on the basis of crafts alone, barring unskilled laborers (as the AFL favored), would allow corporation owners to divide and enfeeble the union movement. Beyond that, I knew little, and I wondered why Sadie would raise this now.

"Your people were Wobblies," she went on. "They called themselves Wobblies because they believed with everything they had that their radicalism would wobble the earth on its axis, that they could shake and then bring down capitalism. Of course, they were mistaken, and, of course, that bum Stalin ruined any chance for the Wobbly ideal of One Big Union."

"My people?"

97

"My *shul,* my house of worship, wasn't, as it was for most Jews, on Saturdays. When I was a young girl in Paterson, my weekly service meant being taken to union rallies on Sunday mornings—or any other day of the week. The rallies happened at the factories all the time back then. I was brought every week to watch my father and grandfather—your people—throw rocks at cops and scabs and then be hauled off to jail."

"A weekly ritual."

"Yes. For your great-grandfather, his father and uncles, and their brothers and cousins, yes—a rite. At first it was frightening. After a while, I knew they'd all be home by dinnertime, at least most days. They'd share tales of the fight. The good fight. So, Jon, when your new son is not taking up as much of your time as he will for the next several years, find out more about your family. They were heroes, Jon. They lost; and they were heroes."

Sadie told me to study up on fallen Wobbly heroes and heroines such as the murdered Joe Hill and Mary Harris ("Mother") Jones. I have the time now, and the impetus. I've amassed a small Kindle library on the Wobblies, and a New Jersey cousin has sent me some very, very old resources.

Sadie said the Wobblies lost, and, of course, on one level that's so. They lost in the sense that the AFL-CIO gradually drew in the IWW's membership and muted the Wobblies' most radical positions. And yet the Wobblies were a powerful impetus to the larger movement that brought us humane child labor laws, the forty-hour workweek, overtime pay, and safety regulations for plants, mines, and fields. And the Wobblies were prominent among the Progressive groups that, in large measure, moved Teddy Roosevelt to propose universal health care. One hundred years on, we're closer than we've ever been to that economic and moral necessity.

So, I've been reading, for Sadie and for myself. I'm getting to know these heroes, my people.

Insubordinate: Refusing to Smack Kids with a Paddle

1991 - 2011

In the late 1980s, my wife Tamar and I moved from Vermont to Las Vegas to be with her folks as her dad battled and beat cancer. I also needed work, and Clark County Schools were hiring quicker than casinos collect sad sack cash. I taught English and history, earning high-level evaluations.

At year's end, I got a call from an assistant superintendent asking me to be a dean at a new suburban high school. He called it the "flagship of the system." When I visited the campus that afternoon, I should have been less impressed than I was by the school's gorgeous architectural use of desert light, its boulders serving as art, its curved glass-and-stone walls. Earlier that day, I should have listened to my roiled gut when the guy said that "Jews like you and me" should be better represented in the newer suburban schools, where "many minority students are bused in because of the courts."

I hated the work from jump. It was clear from the late-summer briefings that my real job was to do my best to keep white, black, Asian, and Hispanic kids as separated as I could in the halls and in the enormous student parking lot, and that a very effective way to do that would be to suspend as many minority kids as I could for as many days at a time as I could get away with. Needless to say, that advice wasn't explicit. But I hadn't been born the day before in the

99

Elvis Presley Memorial Maternity Ward, either. While I don't know of anything as lawsuit-inviting as an actual minority-kid-suspension quota, my stats were checked weekly, and I was soon told by an assistant principal that my September numbers—my disciplinary decisions as a dean—weren't very good.

On my first day, I'd been presented with a paddle and told to use it "as often as necessary." When my eyebrows shot up, the assistant principal shot back a you're-the-wimp-o'-the-world smirk. She pointed out that the paddle had holes in it, a result, she said, of complaints from parents and lawyers, and that "it doesn't really hurt as much as they say." I should have walked out.

I did leave a month or so on. I'd been written up a few times for "reluctance to suspend when it was called for" and for "reluctance to employ" my paddle—and for another violation considered more serious.

• • •

On an October afternoon, I looked up from my computer to see a very tall, well-built Latino boy in my outer office. I'd seen him around. Guillermo was eighteen, a senior, and in the halls at any rate, pretty mild-mannered. I motioned him inside. He handed me a slip and sat down. His math teacher had bounced him for "crude language" and "starting an altercation." He seemed fairly relaxed.

G: He says I called a boy *hijo de puta*. And that I spit at the bastard.

Me: And?

G: I did.

I waited.

G (with some urgency now): Sure I did, Mr. W. He's been touching my sister in the halls. I told him to stop. He....

100

Me: You didn't hit the guy? It says here...how long has he been hitting on Angela?

G: Sure, I hit the guy but before the bell rang and I was in my seat when the bell rang. Angela...he's been bothering her for two weeks. Touching her. I told him to leave her the fuck alone. Look. If I told my *father*...if Angela told *him*....

Me: I understand. Who is it?

G: Eldridge. Jason Eldridge.

Me: Wide receiver?

G: I know teachers see it. They won't send his ass in here 'cause he plays, you know, and you'd have to suspend his ass and it's the season. Makes me real mad. He's not even that good.

Me: The slip says you hit the guy. It really doesn't matter that you hit him before the bell, Guillermo, you know that. The teacher apparently saw you hit the guy.

G (smiling): I know. His tooth's loose.

Me: Well. You know I've got to keep you after for detention. And a suspension may have to follow once I get a more complete story.

G: Damn! This *is* the complete story, Mr. W.! And I can't do any damned detention!

Me: That's the deal, Guillermo. You know that.

G: I'm sorry but I can't. Can't *be* here!

Me: Guillermo....

Guillermo bent forward and rolled up his right jean leg and showed me his electronic bracelet.

G: I can't sit for no damned detention after school.

Me: You mean you have to be home at a certain time?

G: Yeah. 3:30. We're outa here 2:40. I gotta run from the bus stop home or I get in real trouble. I want this to be *over*, man! Damn! My uncle, he has a job for me after high school. He paints houses. But not if I get in more trouble. He says....

Me: What'd you do?

G: 7-Eleven.

Me: 7-Eleven....You stole stuff from a...?

G: We robbed it. Jose hit the guy and took the money and beat him pretty bad. I was stupid to go with him. It was my father's gun he used. Jose's got a record. This was my first time and I wasn't eighteen yet, so I got probation. Jose, he's in prison.

Me: You're on probation, though.

G: Yeah. I was stupid.

Me: I have to....

G: I told you, man, I *can't*....

He rose from his chair, leaning forward. I raised a palm and motioned for him to sit back down. Somewhat to my surprise, he did, but he was no longer at all relaxed. I asked Guillermo for his parole officer's name and number. I called the woman, explained my situation, asked for an extra two hours that afternoon on Guillermo's behalf, and got it. It seemed simple enough. Guillermo, though, was

102

stunned at his P.O.'s flexibility. He extended a hand to me before he left. .

I checked downstairs later with the detention monitor; Guillermo had showed up.

• • •

Two mornings later, I was called to my assistant principal's office. She told me not to sit down; this would be quick. She'd received a call, she said, from Guillermo's mom, thanking her for the help the school had given her son the other afternoon. The assistant principal went on to say that I was not dean material. She rambled a bit, but the idea was that accommodating Guillermo as I'd done was likely to encourage him to want to stay in this school and didn't I understand that just wasn't the right thing for "boys like him"?

Maybe she meant Hispanic boys; maybe she meant boys in trouble with the law. Maybe both. In any case, she was pretty angry that what I'd done had pleased Guillermo's family.

"You had the paddle," she added, "and you blew that, too." She said she bet I never used it. I told her she was right, that I hadn't—as she could see by looking at my write-ups—and that I wouldn't. She nearly spat as she said that I was to be "just a teacher again" at another high school. She had already arranged the transfer. Getting what I *"really* deserved, thrown out on your can," she said, would require her to "deal with jackasses in the union" and she had "better things to do." I cleared out my desk. I took the paddle.

A week on, I got a call from my fellow Jew, the higher-up in central administration who'd initially placed me. He told me I'd "dealt a real blow to Jews" in Clark County Schools, that I embarrassed him personally, that he considered me insubordinate for, among other decisions, not using the "means of corporal punishment" at my disposal. I "shouldn't expect any more favors," he added.

"Shalom," I said, with as much cloying honey in my voice as I could muster. Then I hung up—and mailed him the paddle that afternoon.

Note: Names in this piece have been changed to preserve the privacy of those involved. I am pleased to say that Nevada schools no longer resort to physical punishment.

The United Voice of Torah and Gospel Justice

1993 - 2012

Around 1993, I began to study—in addition to my then longstanding readings in Jewish history and ethics—the work of historians specializing in historical-Jesus research. I wanted to better understand the man, to locate him in his time and place and in what I believe he would have considered his own Jewish tradition, a long line of socially concerned ethical thinkers and prophets.

Nearly twenty years on, what I've learned has helped me better gauge contemporary religious leaders, the worthwhile majority as well as those whose behavior betrays religious or ethical mandates. It has also helped me more firmly grasp the context of the criticism, reflected below, that socially conscious Jewish and Christian clerics and activists lodge against secular and spiritual leaders who fall so far short of the mark.

The Challenge

"Your budget appears to reflect the values of your favorite philosopher, Ayn Rand, rather than the Gospel of Jesus Christ." — from an April 2012 letter to House Budget Committee Chair Paul

Ryan, signed by ninety faculty members and Catholic priests at Georgetown University[1]

"To roll back tax credits for the poor to help fund tax breaks for the rich is morally reprehensible." —Rev. Jim Wallis, president and CEO of the Christian social justice organization Sojourners[2]

"We may not ignore an individual's need for food, clothing or housing; at the same time, we cannot focus only on band-aid solutions to the point that we forget about the grand vision of creating a world without poverty." —Rabbi Jill Jacobs, Executive Director of Rabbis for Human Rights/North America[3]

Twenty-Five Ancient Responses to the Challenge

1. Proverbs 22:16 — "He who oppresses the poor to increase his riches, and he who gives to the rich, will surely come to poverty."

2. Amos 5:11-12 — "Therefore because you trample on the poor and you exact taxes of grain from him, you have built houses of hewn stone, but you shall not dwell in them; you have planted pleasant vineyards, but you shall not drink their wine. For I know how many are your transgressions and how great are your sins—you who afflict the righteous, who take a bribe, and turn aside the needy in the gate."

3. Amos 8:4-7 — "You who cheat and swallow up the needy, and

[1] Laurie Goodstein, "Georgetown Faculty Latest to Chide Ryan," The Caucus Blog, *New York Times,* April 24, 2012.
[2] Sojourners, "Jim Wallis' Statement on Republican Budget," August 1, 2012, http://sojo.net/press/jim-wallis-statement-republican-budget
[3] Jill Jacobs, "Fighting Poverty in Judaism," *My Jewish Learning,* 2010, http://mobile.myjewishlearning.com/practices/Ethics/Caring_For_Ot hers/Social_Welfare/Fighting_Poverty.shtml

make the poor of the land fail, I will never forget what you have done."

4. The Talmud on charity — "We are obligated to be careful with the commandment to give to the poor more than with any other commandment, for charity and justice are the signs of righteousness."

5. The Talmud on charity — "Learning Torah without charity and kindness to the poor is meaningless."

6. Deuteronomy 15:7-8 — "If there is among you a poor man of your brethren...you shall not harden your heart nor shut your hand from your poor brother, but you shall open your hand wide to him and willingly lend him sufficient for his need, whatever he needs."

7. The Talmud on giving to the poor — "You shall give to the needy; your heart should not be grieved when you give."

8. Deuteronomy 15:11 —"For the poor will never cease from the land; therefore I command you, saying, 'You shall open your hand wide to your brother, to your poor and your needy, in your land.'"

9. Proverbs 17:5 — "He who mocks the poor reproaches his Maker; he who is glad at calamity will not go unpunished."

10. Matthew 19:21 — "Jesus said to him, 'If you wish to be perfect, go, sell your possessions and give the money to the poor...then come, follow me.'"

11. Ezekiel 16:49 — "This was the sin of Sodom: she and her daughters had pride, excess of food, and prosperous ease, but did not aid the poor and needy."

12. Proverbs 16:8 — "Better to have a little with righteousness than to have vast revenues without justice."

13. Psalm 82:3 — "Defend the poor and fatherless; do justice to the afflicted and needy."

14. Deuteronomy 24:19-21 — "When you are harvesting in your field and you overlook a sheaf, do not go back to get it. Leave it for the stranger, the orphan, and the widow. When you beat the olives from your trees, do not go over the branches a second time. Leave what remains for the stranger, the orphan, and the widow. When you harvest the grapes in your vineyard, do not go over the vines again. Leave what remains for the stranger, the orphan, and the widow."

16. Exodus 23:11 — "During the seventh year, let the land rest and lie fallow, so that the poor of your people may eat."

17. Leviticus 23:22 — "When you reap the harvest of your land, do not reap to the very edges of your field or gather the gleanings of your harvest. Leave them for the poor and the stranger."

18. Exodus 22:25 — "If you lend money to one who is needy, charge him no interest."

19. Luke 6:20-21 — "Blessed are you who are poor, for yours is the kingdom of God. Blessed are you who are hungry, for you shall be filled. Blessed are you who weep, for you shall laugh."

20. Luke 4:16-19 — "He has anointed me to bring good news to the poor. He has sent me to proclaim release to the captives and recovery of sight to the blind, to let the oppressed go free."

21. Matthew 25:34-36 — "Come...inherit the kingdom prepared for you from the foundation of the world; for I was hungry and you gave me food, I was thirsty and you gave me something to drink, I was a stranger and you welcomed me, I was naked and you gave me clothing, I was sick and you took care of me. I was in prison and you visited me."

22. Mark 10:21-22 — "Jesus said, 'You lack one thing; go, sell what you own, and give the money to the poor...then come, follow me.'"

23. Matthew 25:40 — "Jesus said, 'What you did to the least of my brethren, you did to me.'"

24. The Talmud — "You must teach as God teaches, without collecting a fee."

25. Rabbi Hillel — "This is the whole of Torah law: That which is detestable to you do not do to others."

Any questions? (I hope so.)

Note:

Torah comprises the five books of the written Jewish Law, which parallel the Christian Old Testament:

In/At the Beginning (Genesis)

Now, These Are the Names of the Sons of Israel (Exodus)

And He Called (Leviticus)

In The Wilderness (Numbers)

These Are the Words that Moses Spoke (Deuteronomy)

Talmud is the medieval multi-volume rabbinic commentary on all aspects of the Torah. It is often referred to as the Oral Law (although it is, and has been for ages now, written down).

The Crayon of Color
1994 - 2011

I prefer direct speech to politically correct language and euphemisms. The latter make me itch.

In 1994, I was a candidate to lead the middle division of a venerable pre-K-through-12 independent school in Philadelphia, my hometown. I got the post (and stayed five years) but not before three days of pretty grueling interviews. One day's set included a classroom tour led by the retiring division head, Ms. G. She was intelligent, an accomplished teacher, and a widely published writer in education theory and practice. She led a terrific division in a great school founded in the seventeenth century and long regarded for academic excellence and progressive pedagogical and social commitments.

But even laudable missions can be expressed absurdly and to ends that escape understanding.

I accompanied the outgoing director to classes in algebra, art, history, geography, and science and to writing lessons. A fifth grade group was drawing pictures to illustrate stories they had written based on literature they'd read and discussed. From what I saw, the children's stories and pictures were all at least interesting and some were just terrific.

Each child had his or her own box of Crayolas and dozens of pages of blank paper. As we approached one desk, my host encouragingly addressed a ten-year-old girl: "Sara, I love how you're using subtle tones and hues."

110

The girl smiled.

"And, Sara, I'm impressed with how you've used your lemon for plain yellow on these bumble bees. That's creative! And you've made excellent use of..." —she smiled as she then picked up the black stick—"...your crayon of color."

It took every facial muscle drawn taut, every bit of control I could summon, to steady my eyes, keep them within a foot of my face. But she saw my jaw move, and her own mouth tightened. She said in a new tone, one I might more have expected from a Red Guard in a Maoist political reeducation camp, "That. Is. What. We. Call. It. Here. It. Is. The. Crayon. Of. Color."

With some difficulty, I refrained from asking what the brown, tan, and red crayons were called. But when I took hold of the Middle Division the following fall, we called them the brown, tan, and red (and black) crayons.

"Fully and Completely Weaned"

1995 - 2010

Among the reasons I moved from teaching only to joint teaching/administration is that deans, division heads, and heads of schools have many more opportunities to problem solve with families. My administrative role enabled me to know families far more intimately than I had before and afforded me many chances to make immediate, broad, and lasting differences in their lives. I was thrilled to add these occasions to the joy I'd already found sharing content, skills, and my excitement in the humanities.

The role of a division head, dean, or head of school is relatively open; aside from the hour each day that we may teach (a welcome hour of relative predictability), we're trying to shape lives in a continually moving, unpredictable, bubble-up environment. Whatever's on your slate can easily be upended, even at the very end of a day.

The most terrible and unique interruption happened to all of us on 9/11, when two of the students at my school—twin sixth grade boys—lost their dad on the plane that flew into the Pentagon.

Yet, disruptions to schedules occur for far less harrowing reasons, such as a sudden, mid-morning teacher illness; pranks that explode toilets; pranks in which candy bars are chucked into toilets, then offered to the candyless at lunch (middle school boys have a singular affinity with toilets); unexpected, suspendable behavior by an athlete on the eve of a championship; and plagiarism, cheating, or

112

drug allegations just prior to college admissions decisions. These and many more conspire to overturn any sense of planning.

My strangest unexpected moment, however, was not in any way public, involved no rule breaking, did not threaten anyone on or off campus, and didn't affect routine.

It upended only me.

Late on a grey, cold Philadelphia November day—the air outside crisply pregnant with winter's certain coming—as the students were just leaving our very old and justifiably respected Quaker private school in the center of town, I returned to my Middle School Division Head's office from rounds of shared Friday afternoon goodbyes with maintenance people, students, and colleagues.

I placed my books and papers together and was rising from my chair when a tall, sharp-featured woman with very long, thick silver-and-black hair brushed severely up and back to one side of her head blew into my office, chin jutting. She wore an open, black canvas duster with silver snaps over a navy crew sweater. The coat fell to the ankles of black corduroy jeans.

I recognized her as the mother of a fourteen-year-old boy who had come to us that fall from the West Coast. Reports suggested that Billy had been doing reasonably well, academically and socially. His mother and I hadn't seen each other since a soccer match two months ago, where we'd said hello.

I had barely extended my hand, just got out the words, "Good afternoon, Ms. Parker; how may I...?" when she drew herself up within an inch of my face and announced in a voice that sounded as if it had been etched by heavy shards of glass: "I would like you to know, sir, that I stopped breastfeeding William last summer, and, despite what his father in Seattle may tell you, William is now weaned. Fully and completely weaned. I am confident we will not soon see him returning to the breast."

She turned and swept from the room.

113

Note: Names in this piece have been changed to preserve the privacy of those involved.

My Bum Kidneys: Far Too Alone in My Luck

1998 - 2010

I'm lucky.

I knew—as hundreds of thousands of Americans know about themselves—that I'd need a new kidney. I'm far luckier than most, because I also knew what most don't: I'd never have to do dialysis, and I'd never be waiting on a recipient list. My sister had offered me a kidney. We did the switch-out on July Fourth weekend, 1998; we'd arranged it long in advance. The sense of control in an otherwise unsettling time was palpable and welcome.

The overwhelming number of people who need a new kidney never have the luxury we had. Some resort to obtaining illicit organs. A worldwide black market flourishes—and hardly just in kidneys. Most often, donors in poor nations (and rundown American and other first-world neighborhoods) get a pittance for their organs after extraction under conditions that are often remarkably filthy.

There's no comprehensive solution to the awful ratio of supply to demand for transplants, yet Richard Thaler, a professor of economics and behavioral science at the University of Chicago, offered an interesting potential route in a September 2009 *New York Times* article, "Opting in vs. Opting Out."[1]

---

[1] Richard Thaler, "Opting in vs. Opting Out," *New York Times,* September 26, 2009.

He points out that here in America we use an opt-in donor model: you check off on your driver's license if you want your organs to live on after you. A number of countries, including France, Belgium, Finland, Denmark, Italy, Spain, Norway, and Sweden[2], have gone to an opt-out model, in which your consent is presumed. All citizens are expected to be donors (unless, of course, it would be medically unwise for a specific individual).

In survey after survey, most Americans support organ donation, yet donation rates remain very low. In countries with presumed consent laws, only five percent opt out. There's no guarantee that universal presumed consent would eliminate the black market, but the record does show that, in the countries that presume donor consent, legitimate availability has increased significantly.

I follow the medical debates and related news on the issue, including the intermittent arrests and trials of those who (you'll excuse the expression) gouge the poor to make enormous profits on their body parts.

The opt-out model for organ donation is the first ray of light I've seen. We should explore it. Remarkably few with bum kidneys have been as lucky as I am, and I dislike feeling so alone in my luck.

---

[2] "Opt-Out versus Opt-in Donation Systems," Mount Holyoke College Organ Transplantation website,
http://pub.mtholyoke.edu/journal/Organ/entry/opt_out_versus_opt_in

My African-American Son Owns the Confederate Flag; I Wish I Could

1999 - 2011

A Confederate battle flag greeted my family in an upscale Atlanta suburb a few days after we moved in, in 1999. The elderly couple across the street, originally from South Carolina, stuck it on a pole on their lawn when they realized that the black child playing outside was not a stray from a distant neighborhood but our son. To our then nine-year-old's immense credit—and I heard this story from him only years on—he decided to make a foray across the street, introduce himself to the couple, and ask if he could use the rusted basketball hoop in their drive. They agreed that he could, and, a month later, the flag was gone.

Our son's always had that way about him.

Today, in 2013, that flag remains aloft at the South Carolina State House, along with the flag of the United States—my flag, the one that defeated the Confederacy. The governor of the state, Nikki Haley, a person of mixed racial heritage herself, has been asked to remove the Confederate battle flag from the State Capitol but refuses to discuss the matter.

The Stars and Stripes defeated the Stars and Bars. Or did it?

When in history has another nation so thoroughly coddled the memory and so painstakingly memorialized the iconic relics and ideology of a 150-year-old, morally bankrupt and illegal rebellion against itself? You cannot find one.

117

Then why have we done it?

You know the answer. And so does my son, a championship marksman and a young man considering a career in military service to his country. Yet, incredibly, he's made a far better, if uneasy, peace with the answer than I ever will.

I envy him.

Bleach in His Face: A Rabbi Exposes Sexual Abuse in His Ultra-Orthodox Community

1963 - 2000 - 2013

When, of a Friday afternoon in late November 1963, I made my stunned and miserable way home from junior high, my weeping mother greeted me at our front door. She wrapped me in her arms and, to my naive twelve-year-old disbelief, whispered, "Jonny, I hope it wasn't a Jew who shot him."

Now, my mother was the granddaughter of New York Jewish leftists, radical unionists, members of the Industrial Workers of the World. She was, perhaps, the least traditionally religious person I knew. Yet, she was born in 1928. As a child, she likely heard the stories of the Eastern European pogroms against the Jews, and, as a teen, she was undoubtedly aware of Jewish genocide during the Second World War. It affected her. The sensibility she carried even as a decidedly secular Jew, her utterance to me that horrific afternoon—it remains with me.

• • •

In December 2012, Rabbi Nuchem Rosenberg was violently assaulted by a fellow Jew in a longstanding Ultra-Orthodox Jewish community, the Williamsburg section of Brooklyn. As related in a *New York Times* article by Sharon Otterman[7], the assailant

---

[7] Sharon Otterman, "Chemical Thrown at Rabbi Who Aided Victims of Abuse," *New York Times,* December 11, 2012.

apparently stalked the rabbi for some distance and then, on Roebling Street at around noon, threw a cup of bleach in the rabbi's face. Rabbi Rosenberg was treated at a nearby hospital and released; he'll recover fully.

What did Rabbi Rosenberg do to merit bleach in the face?

The answer goes to the sometimes dark heart of what it means to live as an Ultra-Orthodox Jew in America—perhaps to live as a tiny, and often frightened, minority anywhere.

I first thoroughly understood what it might mean in 2000. I was the administrator in charge of secular studies at an Orthodox Jewish day school. While devout, the rabbis who taught there—my colleagues—were not what would be called Ultra-Orthodox. They and their families lived to a significant extent in agreeable concert with the outside world. In no sense was their community cut off from the surrounding suburban or city life. To this secular Jew, they seemed to me to have struck a fair balance without diluting their religious or civic responsibilities or commitments.

So it surprised me at first when my colleagues met Connecticut Senator Joe Lieberman's 2000 vice presidential candidacy with forceful rejection—and not without fear. I soon realized that my colleagues were more concerned by Mr. Lieberman's pragmatic self-identification as an Orthodox Jew than by his then modest liberal voting record. Any pride that may have arisen from a religious Jew ascending to those political heights, any sense that "we made it," was overwhelmed by the fear that were Mr. Leiberman, as vice president or as a potential president, to have any serious failures in office, Jews everywhere would bear the consequences. When the Court finally settled *Bush v. Gore*, even the few rather progressive rabbis with whom I taught sighed with profound relief.

One further preliminary before I explain why Rabbi Rosenberg was attacked in Brooklyn:

Several years back, I wrote a series of pieces on the now justly imprisoned Iowa rabbi, Shlomo Rubashkin, one-time manager of the world's largest kosher slaughterhouse/meat-packing plant. When Iowa and the feds went after Rabbi Rubashkin—for, among other offenses, bank fraud and hundreds of violations of child labor laws, illegally importing Mexican workers to work and live under horrid conditions for substandard wages—some in the American Ultra-Orthodox communities petitioned widely and used the considerable political influence they had to try to free the rabbi outright.

Although his subsequent trial brought out a shamefully squalid sequence of wrongdoing, including the fact that when the FBI snatched him up he was preparing to flee to Israel, those same people in the same communities worked hard to get his sentence limited to the minimum term. As it turned out, Rabbi Rubashkin was given his due, an appropriately long sentence in federal prison. (I'm pleased to note that a solid majority of American Jews, including many Orthodox Jews, were pleased with the results of the trial.) The forty-something may or may not get out in time for a granddaughter's wedding.

Now, back to Brooklyn.

Rabbi Rosenberg's attacker, the bleach hurler, was just one of tens of thousands of Ultra-Orthodox Jews who reviled the rabbi for aiding the Brooklyn District Attorney in 2012 in bringing to justice another man from their community. The now convicted fellow had promoted himself as a counselor to wayward teens. He was just found guilty in a Brooklyn court of sexually abusing a teenage girl from the community over a three-year period.

Rabbi Rosenberg maintains a website and a call-in line for any young person in the community who believes s/he has been abused. He was initially contacted in this way by the girl in the court case. The whistle-blowing rabbi's problem was that he violated a longstanding unwritten rule of many Ultra-Orthodox communities: He did not allow the community to deal with the girl's accusations itself, insulated from secular authority. Not reporting abuse or other

121

crimes has been the norm. Rabbi Rosenberg, by contrast, understood that whatever responsibilities he had to his religious community, his personal and professional responsibility to the girl who came forward to him—and his civic responsibility to the People of New York—outweighed the demand for insularity.

I do understand the fears of this tiny religious minority. They are my people, my fellow Jews, despite the fact that my Jewish life bears little resemblance to theirs. Yet, my mother's sensibilities, and my own, force me to understand these people, even while I cannot possibly concur with their behavior in these circumstances.

The predator's conviction and the girl's vindication are for the good. Justice won here. I celebrate the guts of this child and the courage of Rabbi Nuchem Rosenberg who knew the risks awaiting him should the girl's abuser be tried and convicted. I long for my people's Ultra-Orthodox communities to show a broader understanding of what justice demands, despite their sometimes understandable fears of the larger world they inhabit with us.

9/11: Telling Small Twins Their Dad Was on the Plane

2001 - 2011

I did not—any more than most of you—suffer on that morning, and I suffered much less than some of you. In fact, "suffer" is too strong a word for me. No one I immediately knew was in the towers, on the planes. I don't for a moment see myself in the emotional pool of people who knew them, loved them.

But I did have a sudden, wrenching job to do that morning—and it abides with me.

I was working then as Middle School Division Head at a 700-student independent school in Washington's northwest Maryland suburbs, and I'd set aside early Tuesday mornings for a weekly meeting with the guidance staff. The eighty-acre campus welcomes students from eight through eighteen; our middle school had then perhaps 175 children, housed in a venerable stone-and-brick two-story building, solid, yet warmly inviting.

The Georgian architecture, the elaborate jungle gyms, the lawns, the lacrosse fields and the ball diamonds, the overall stateliness of the place greeted me that morning as it had every morning since I'd begun there a month before. Even the crisp air and beautiful azure sky felt welcoming.

It was a trick.

Fifteen minutes into my weekly guidance meeting, my wife Tamar called to tell me of the initial attacks on the World Trade Center. I thanked her, told her I loved her and that I'd be home when it made sense to be home, that I'd be in touch throughout the day, that our son Graham's school would keep children safe (did I know that?). I told my guidance people, who then rushed from the room. There would be frightened children to see, and none of us knew how soon or how many.

Our weekly all-school meeting at the gymnasium was luckily scheduled to begin in twenty minutes, so I walked over, meeting the headmaster on the footpath. The athletic director had his television on in his office off the gym, but the enormous, empty space was otherwise unsettlingly quiet. The headmaster asked me to remain on the gym floor to see to any arriving students while he checked the news in the director's office. He came back out quickly to tell me about the assault on the Pentagon, twenty-some minutes south. He said, calmly, "Jon, our country's under attack."

Students arrived now, many of whom had fathers, mothers, uncles, aunts, and older siblings working in New York, on Wall Street, and elsewhere. Some of these parents and other relatives commuted to Manhattan from Washington. Some students had relatives at the Pentagon.

Cell phones began beeping and kept on throughout our abbreviated assembly, where the headmaster—without alarm in his tone or pulling any punches—told the children just what happened at the Pentagon and in lower Manhattan. He said that the United States was attacked by as-yet-unknown persons, that we did not know if the attacks were finished, and that we did not know if we were at war or not. He told lower and middle school students that they could leave if their parents signed them out. Upper school students, including those who drove to school, could leave or stay but were required to sign out if they left. In fact, very few parents came for their children early, and the older students apparently felt better on campus in one another's company.

124

After heading back to my office, I visited most classrooms, having instructed teachers to turn televisions off by 11:00. There was, we knew, nothing new to be seen, just an endless, horrifying, fiery loop. Talk was encouraged; watching the same scenes of destruction over and again was unnecessary.

The headmaster's call came as I got to my desk: "Jon, in ten minutes, Mrs. Goldman and her rabbi will be at your office. The twins' dad was on the plane at the Pentagon. Good luck. Bad, bad day, Jon." He hung up.

The twins were Ricky and Saul, sixth graders.

I told my secretary what was about to happen and that I'd be asking her to collect the twins from class.

Molly was a sturdy woman, with years and years of private school staff experience. She'd seen tons, but not this. No one had. She cried, then took hold of herself and said, "I'm all right, Jon." I'd known Molly just a month, having arrived in August myself. I walked around her desk and hugged her hard.

"You look calm, Jon," she said. "Stay that way, please."

I remember asking myself if I was as calm as I seemed. Whatever my appearance, I know I was roiling inside.

Molly announced the rabbi a few minutes later, and he led in Mrs. Goldman and another woman, a close friend. Mrs. Goldman's self-possession was immediately apparent and astonishing under the circumstances. She spoke as she took her seat, telling us that her husband took that flight from Dulles once each month. What she wanted, now, was to be present when her boys were told.

I asked Molly to get the boys. They'd know what had happened as soon as they were called for (if they hadn't known it inside themselves already), but we decided it would be worse were any of us to accompany Molly. When Ricky and Saul came in, they began

125

crying softly as soon as they saw their mom and their rabbi. No one spoke for half a minute. Mrs. Goldman stroked her sons' hair and knees. She held their hands. Her eyes conveyed all that needed to be said.

Nonetheless, the rabbi looked at me, nodding. I said, "Boys, as you've realized, your dad was on that plane. We are all so sorry." They cried and cried. They moaned and buried their heads in their mom's chest. They'd seen their dad that morning. He'd hugged them goodbye. He was off to Dulles, and they were off to school. The rabbi stood and, with his arm around Mrs. Goldman's shoulders, bent down and whispered to the boys.

After they left, I did one more round of the classrooms and told teachers what had happened. I trusted all of them to handle our horrid news with grace. I did not think it made sense to try to keep this from students when the middle school grapevine is, as you know, more effective than any formal adult announcement. At the next change of classes, Molly collected the boys' books from their classrooms.

I called Tamar. She seemed okay. I called our son's middle school and after four tries, got through. All the kids were fine.

Later, on my way home—after my faculty and I met parents in the parking lots—I drove, as I always did, by a government-owned conference center (ostensibly a postal worker training facility) on the grounds of a gorgeous, beige-stone former monastery. Two black SUVs were parked where the road met the conference center's incredibly long, snaky driveway. Two black-suited agents in sunglasses, a man and a woman, stood by, holding automatic rifles.

At home, Tamar, Graham, and I sat on a soft couch. We held our son, and we slept together on that couch until long after dark.

Note: Names in this piece have been changed to preserve the privacy of those involved.

I Helped Tear a Family Apart to Save an Autistic Boy

2004 - 2010

The odds are higher than ever that you know a child struggling with autism.

In 2008, the Centers for Disease Control and Prevention looked at records of 400,000 kids nationwide.[1] The study found that diagnoses of all forms of autism are increasing at remarkable rates. In 2000, the number was 1 in 300. By 2007, it had risen to 1 in 150. In March 2012, the CDC reported that the incidence rate had increased to 1 in 88.[2]

The reports put me in mind of one of the saddest and most wrenching decisions I ever made in a long career as an administrator in private schools. And yet my decision to exit Teddy from his school in 2003 was not only heartbreaking but right.

Twelve years old, red haired and handsome, Teddy had been initially (and properly) diagnosed with severe autism, but our admissions people had been told by his psychologist that his was, at

---

[1] "Prevalence of Autism Spectrum Disorders — Autism and Developmental Disabilities Monitoring Network, 14 Sites, United States, 2008," Centers for Disease Control and Prevention, March 30, 2012.

[2] "New Data on Autism Spectrum Disorders," Centers for Disease Control and Prevention, March 29, 2012.

worst, a mild case, and that he could handle the rigors of a top-flight, traditional independent school—even one, like ours, that didn't have teachers trained in any way to help him to integrate, succeed, and be happy.

While Teddy was academically very bright, after a grueling two-month struggle to make it work, it became clear that the tantrums without apparent provocation, the screaming at staff, the taunts of girls and boys and teachers alike, the serious time spent most days in the Guidance Office and with me, and the many early dismissals into his mother's care, we had to consider a change.

Ironically—and in a way this saddened me even more—his one-on-ones with me when he just could not cope with groups of fifteen or twenty peers, were pleasant. We talked about baseball, science, books he'd read. We played chess and a variation of *Go*, the Japanese board game of territorial acquisition played with white and black stones. And we talked about his perceived "enemies"—his word—adults and kids.

I'm no therapist and I've never pretended to be, yet it became clear that a one-to-one situation, or at least, say, a three- or four-to-one, was what Teddy needed every day. He never raised his voice in my office, and he tried to make eye contact more than a few times.

Yet, a second struggle, now daily, became layered over the first, this one with Teddy's family. His three older brothers had graduated from our school, as had his dad, who was desperate for him to complete the family cycle. But Teddy's lack of common social skills, inability to pick up on cues from adults and peers, tendency to become overwhelmed in groups greater than five or six, and inability to act within an acceptable range of behaviors made school life increasingly miserable for him. Our recommendation to transfer him from our school split his dad from his eventually more reasonable mom, and I have no doubt contributed to their eventual separation.

We recommended a school far better equipped for autistic children than we were, both in mission and in program. Its faculty members were appropriately trained. After a three-month painful push and pull with the family and his psychologist—we did not want to expel the child, as he'd have had to explain that from a defensive posture for years—Teddy withdrew from our school, enrolled in the new one, and thrived. The new school's staff diagnosed him with a particularly tough form of autism, well along the spectrum.

Our relationship with Teddy's parents had soured beyond repair and so had his parents' relationship with one another, but we had served him (and our other students) well.

Dr. Catherine Rice, a behavioral health scientist with the CDC's National Center on Birth Defects and Developmental Disabilities, said in a December 2009 press briefing[3] that she isn't certain why such a sharp increase in autism has occurred. No single, simple explanation is apparent. Diagnoses may reflect increased symptom awareness, sparked by advocacy groups, or, perhaps, the disorder is in fact increasingly more common.

Still, a doubled diagnosis rate over seven years is not something reasonable people dismiss as somehow driven by politics or advocacy groups, as some media commentators claim. The radio talk show host Michael Savage does, and to no end; others have aped his dismissive, venal hate. They contend that parents of these kids simply want your money, while avoiding responsibility for what is no more than poor parenting.

More serious study needs to be done so that children whose conditions fall within the range we call autism will have a better shot at living happier lives and contributing as effectively as possible to family, community, and economic life as adults.

---

[3] "CDC Press Briefing on Autism Surveillance Summary," December 18, 2009.

Note: Names in this piece have been changed to preserve the privacy of those involved.

My Crimson Brush with Animal Cruelty

2004 - 2009

The *Harvard Classics*, published in 1910, are a gorgeous fifty-one-volume leather-bound set of books, the Western canon in literature, sciences, philosophy, and the arts. The set I have has, in each of its volumes, the fountain pen signature of its original owner, a woman from New Orleans.

Southern Louisiana is where I found them, following an Internet search that told me a fellow living in a parish fifty miles north of New Orleans had a "book shop in my home" and an original set of *The Classics*. He was willing not only to part with them for an astonishingly small price but willing, too, at his expense, to box and ship all the volumes, with their glorious old-book smell, their sturdy crimson-and-gold bindings intact, and just a few pages frayed.

I have now read many of the books, not in order but following my moods. I have enjoyed again Shakespeare, Plato, Montaigne, St. Augustine—so many thinkers and movers of minds. I'm nowhere near, of course, finished.

I called as well as emailed to make arrangements to buy the books. The seller, a relatively young Southern man by his voice, spoke to me over what was a fair din of barking and howling and a woman calling to dogs, "Come on out back! Supper, y'all!" At the time, I thought nothing of it.

My set arrived within the week, and after the initial thrill of shelving them and deciding which ones to tackle first, I recalled the feverishly barking dogs. I did another Internet search, this time

131

keying not on the collection or the book shop but on the seller's name.

This is what I found.

The booksellers, husband and wife, had been listed (with their address) by several local organizations as being suspected of animal cruelty and were on one organization's "watch list." One post said this couple at one time had well over fifty dogs "of many breeds." These were allegations only and informal—not from any state agency and nothing like an indictment.

Yet, those howls stayed with me.

A year later, having read perhaps half the volumes he'd sent me, I looked up the fellow again. By that point, there had been not only indictments but convictions, and the "book shop in my home" had been shuttered. Shut down, too, was the couple's shabby, soiled three-acre ranch-style property, along with their routine near-starvation of dogs (despite the call to supper I'd heard on the phone).

Among my first thoughts was that I hoped these two had no human children, but I never found out. I didn't want to find out. Neglecting and hurting animals can be a sign that people will neglect and hurt their kids.

A number of states, including California, Colorado, Indiana, Maine, Ohio, and West Virginia, are taking measures to coordinate efforts among animal and child protection agencies.[1] I'm pleased at the tightened coordination and that penalties are now being handed out for even one instance of animal abuse. Those inclined to abuse animals, even once, should not have kids, and there's an argument to be made that the state should remove from the home not only the abused animal but the potentially abused child. In fact, I'd say that a

---

[1] Mary Lou Randour and Howard Davidson, *A Common Bond: Maltreated Children and Animals in the Home* (American Humane, 2008).

132

child—particularly a smaller child—living alongside animal abuse is already abused by what she is forced to witness.

I still cherish my *Harvard Classics*. I wish, though, that their beautiful crimson bindings didn't so sadly recall for me those howling dogs.

"Sweet Jesus, White People Dumb as Shit!"

2005 - 2011

On Halloween night, we watched Lon Chaney's 1931 classic *Frankenstein*. (A Jewish monster? Well, okay. He *does* derive from the golem, an oft-repeated, multiversion story from the old Eastern European Jewry about an animated being created entirely from inanimate matter.) Enjoying *Frankenstein* immensely again, I was put in mind of a unique teaching moment from 2005, one from which I may have learned far more than my students did.

• • •

Most teachers know that the most scrumptious, hilarious, and, often, most meaningful moments aren't anticipated. Sometimes humor, energy, and meaning inadvertently emerge from a student's background, from her set of cultural expectations, which can be just so different from—well, in LaTisha's case—mine.

And, sometimes, what is genuinely funny can seem on first blush crude or even racist, unless one takes into account those divergent cultural histories. This was such a moment, although it may not be one for those who cherish what I'll call cultural symmetry, the unstated demand—often made by majorities—that minorities express themselves as if they've lived life as majorities do. When we make that demand, we miss, or dismiss, some of life's most pungently endearing and important moments.

I'm pleased my students and I didn't miss this one.

134

Before I retired, I taught at a school for kids struggling with dyslexia. Most of the students were intelligent, and when they got this shot at our school, seen by them and their parents as their last good chance, they were determined to make something excellent of it.

LaTisha was a junior, just under five feet and skinny, a stick of fire-eyes dynamite. She was "destined of the Lord" to be a defense attorney, to "take up for people screwed by the Man." I was impressed by her sense of purpose and her use of the phrase "the Man," a term embedded in her parents' and grandparents' world of urban African-Americans more than in her own. LaTisha was also, on occasion, defiant, so I had her sit about sixteen inches across a narrow table from me. I knew her tendency for acting up, and this arrangement tended to blunt it. However, it didn't stop LaTisha from voicing her often unfiltered ideas and feelings, even if *sotto voce*, and I'm (mostly) glad it didn't.

As is commonly known, one way of helping dyslexic kids absorb literature is to choose excellent novels and plays that have been translated to film, because the more senses there are to access plots, themes, and dialogue, the better. Film can palpably enhance reading. That's likely true for most kids, dyslexic or no.

My students loved, for instance, Roman Polanski's remarkably bloody *Macbeth* and Franco Zefferelli's *Romeo and Juliet*, for example, as a preliminary for reading and acting out scenes from Shakespeare. With language-challenged children, voices and bodies in motion help a lot.

From jump, LaTisha could not take seriously the hero and heroine in the 1930s film classic, *The Most Dangerous Game*, based on the 1924 Richard Connell short story. The film, which stars Joel Macrae and Fay Wray, follows the tale: a hero is stranded on a private Atlantic isle owned by an exiled, prerevolutionary Russian baron, a mad big game hunter who, grown bored of bagging boar, tiger, lion, wildebeest, and panther, now arranges mishaps at sea and hunts those who make it to shore.

135

Toward the middle of the film, there's the obligatory goose-bumpy scene when the hero and damsel—wanting to discover the reason why the baron had warned them not to go down, down, down to the dungeon-like basement—creep slowly down the shadowy, windy staircase.

You just know this isn't a good idea.

But, of course, our hero and damsel don't know it's a very *bad* idea—that all sorts of heads, animal and human, are mounted on the dungeon walls. And they creep on. Most audiences see them as bold and brave.

Not LaTisha.

At the precise moment they get midway creepy-creepy-down, LaTisha, shaking her head, said under her breath, "Sweet *Jesus!* White people dumb as shit!"

I began laughing so hard I nearly fell to the floor.

My class, of course, demanded to know what LaTisha had whispered. Still laughing, I stepped to the DVD player, paused the film, and invited LaTisha to let the class in on it. She looked at me very briefly as if to ask, *Is this some teacher trick?,* saw my face, shrugged, and repeated aloud her matter-of-fact assessment of white people heroes and damsels—born to a world so very safe and predictable compared to hers, compared to her parents', compared to her grandparents', that they, white people, would actually creep down that foreboding and so obviously bad-bad-very-bad-idea creepy, windy staircase.

And so, totally unplanned, one of the very best cross-cultural discussions I ever witnessed ensued. LaTisha, and every other black child in that room, certified white people as, yes, *dumb as shit* for not knowing what they said black people, by dint of such a very different, utterly asymmetrical cultural history, just *knew:* No one with an ounce of sense would step down those stairs.

136

Now, extrapolate this lesson to most facets of life, and you have a partial yet salient understanding of LaTisha's world view including that a white kid saying the same about black people would not, simply would not, have been an equivalent demonstration of understanding.

And it would not have been funny, because the demand for cultural symmetry is a wish only majorities cherish and foist upon minorities only, for the most part, in semiconscious fantasy. But fantasy is all it is. The demand for cultural symmetry does not reflect any legitimate or meaningful shared historical or current reality at all.

I'm recalling that moment now: I'm looking at their faces, black and white—smiles and laughter and the excellent exchange of ideas and feeling among us for several days thereafter—and LaTisha assuring us she'd said it "only in the very nicest way."

And then her deliciously ambiguous wink.

For the *Lord of the Flies* Small Mystic, a Response to Clerical Evil

2005 - 2012

"Cardinal Roger M. Mahoney, for more than 25 years the savvy shepherd of the Roman Catholic Church in Los Angeles, retired nearly two years ago…pledging to stay in the spotlight by continuing to fight for the rights of immigrants. But the cardinal now finds himself in a most unwelcome spotlight, one that he sought for years to avoid. Internal church personnel files released this week as part of a civil court case reveal that he and his top advisor knowingly shielded priests accused of child sexual abuse from law enforcement." —Laurie Goodstein, "Sexual Abuse Files Cast Shadow on Los Angeles Cardinal," *New York Times*, January 22, 2013.

"An unlicensed therapist and respected member of an ultra-Orthodox Jewish Community in Brooklyn [Nechemya Weberman] was sentenced on Tuesday to 103 years in prison for repeatedly sexually abusing a young woman, beginning the attacks when she was 12." —Sharon Otterman, "Therapist Sentenced to 103 Years for Sexual Abuse," *New York Times*, January 23, 2013.

It isn't every day that we learn of moral corruption in two major American religious communities. But on consecutive days in January 2013, we did.

The behavior presents a challenge beyond criminal law to those of us, religious or not, who wrestle with and value the books of wisdom of ancient religions. As a writer who studies these Jewish and Christian texts along with the voluminous commentaries on them, hearing so regularly of new charges and court outcomes is an affront. I have found myself falling back on my own reserves as I struggle with the ideas with which these books challenge us, relying less and less for intellectual guidance on religious institutional authorities.

When priests, ministers, rabbis, imams—men who are said to be especially knowledgeable—commit morally corrupt acts, and when these acts seem repeated over and again, I find myself wondering (and I imagine I'm not alone) why I, why many, spend the time that we do trying to grasp complex religious texts. I wonder why any of us should regard Jewish thought or, say, Christology, as any more fundamental to how we live our lives than Hulu reruns of *Gidget* or *The Gong Show*. Ongoing clerical corruption waters the seeds of cynicism that lie fallow in all of us, even those of us who love to wrestle with sacred texts.

And this isn't a problem solely for the religious, for in a world in which fewer and fewer nonreligious people (and I count myself among them) more and more see the benefits of confronting the justice paradigms and view the demands embedded in the texts as hollow. And this holds, I think, for the religious, the agnostic, and for the atheist alike, as I know no one who would choose to live in a world without ethics.

The piling up of report after report like the two I quote from corrodes the incentive to study, to come to know, to reflect on, and then act for the good. The corruption makes the repair of the world, our real work here, seem less promising. If even religious leaders can be corrupt, what hope have we for finding justice anywhere?

139

I've concluded that the only proper response to the corruption—in the face of what could so easily turn me away from my pursuit—is my willful recommitment to study the ancient religious texts in order to do good.

For as William Golding's small, brilliant, and doomed mystic, Simon, knows in his pounding head and within his gorgeous, torn-up, pounding heart after he confronts the core of human evil in the pig's head—subverting every literary Judeo-Christian tradition and expectation of a paradigmatic meeting of a prophet with God on a mountain—"What else is there to do?"[1]

---

[1] William Golding, *Lord of the Flies* (Coward-McCann, 1955).

GREED

2010

(Originally published in slightly different form in *Does This Make Sense?*)

I t is in the nature of evil to overreach. It can't help itself.

This is why justice does, inevitably, dawn; evil is defeated, justice rises up. And the overreach, so often, is in the service of nothing more interesting or special than greed. Yet, greed always undermines evil, creating unintended, untenable consequences for the greedy, and justice eventually triumphs.

I have in mind several seemingly disparate, yet fundamentally connected, American incarnations of the phenomenon.

In 2010, we had front row seats as we watched the House majority vote, in effect, to end Medicare, signaling its intent to reverse the New Deal guarantees to the elderly and the poor. At the time, I was convinced that this unprecedented overreach by those in thrall to insurance conglomerates would ultimately fail. Its demise wouldn't simply be that the Senate wouldn't further it. Its failure would be that of the party itself, when voters recoiled from the idea that the people they elected the previous year would force them in ten years to pay out of pocket for their aging parents' medical care—and later, in their own final years, for their own.

141

Raw ideology can be a moral stigmatism. Raw ideology in the service of greed is blinding, and the blind never see what's coming.

Most Western nations have long since overthrown capital punishment, and it is in increasing disarray here. The 35 states still clinging to the death penalty like starving mutts drawn to rotten meat have been running out of the poisons that do the dirty business. State governments and the pharmaceutical industry, largely to save on labor costs, have depended primarily on the nonunion overseas manufacture and transport of the five drugs used in lethal injections.

That decision has, in delicious irony, proved deadly for capital punishment. With those drugs already in short supply, India and Britain have stopped exporting them, and Britain has strongly urged the European Union to follow suit. In itself, this won't kill the death penalty, but it will save lives; states cannot easily return to electrocutions, firing squads, and hangings.

Retooling capital punishment would take far more than legislative votes. To start, legislatures won't want to invest in defending themselves against challenges based on the Eighth Amendment's guarantee against cruel and unusual punishments. After all, lethal injection was instituted to answer those objections.

This contemporary greed and its unintended consequences have, of course, many historical antecedents. I'll focus on one here.

It's said that slavery is our nation's original sin; I believe that's true.

What really killed slavery—over a decade before the Civil War and emancipation—was the slaveholders' stunningly arrogant greed as expressed in its remarkable overreach, the Fugitive Slave Act of 1850. Prior to that law, which was demanded by every state that was later to secede, the only Northerners prepared to fight over slavery were a distinct minority of deeply committed abolitionists. The Fugitive Slave Act radicalized Northerners because it required the fining and imprisonment of anyone, North or South, found harboring

142

a runaway. Until then, slavery could be (even by well-meaning Northerners) dismissed as a peculiar, if immoral, southern quirk.

The slaveholders' obsessive greed—which created very practical and dire consequences for the average northern farmer who, out of simple decency, might shield a fugitive slave—led to a ramping up of abolitionist feeling in the North that was theretofore unseen. The South's unintended self-destruction of the Confederacy was guaranteed when it forced Congress to pass, and President Fillmore to sign, the Fugitive Slave Act as part of the doomed Missouri Compromise.

Evil always overreaches in the service of greed. That's its nature, eventually to subvert itself. In time it loses, whether the objective was to kill the New Deal's legacy, hold on to the death penalty, or secure and expand slavery. This holds for nearly every other societal sin.

I've no idea when we'll learn.

Ending Affirmative Action

2010

Affirmative action, first coined and developed into policy in the early 1960s, may well have seen its most productive days. Before we say a final goodbye, however, I'd raise two points about when it should end.

I'll be okay with the end of affirmative action based on race (and class) when:

- Medical schools end their age-old admissions preference for children of doctors. Call any med school. If the assistant admissions dean to whom you're passed is honest, she'll tell you that the practice is very much alive and that the school believes it's in the interests of the school's future and of medicine in the United States. And that may be right. What she won't tell you, unless pressed (and she may not even think about this much), is that the children of doctors are overwhelmingly white upper-middles because doctors are, and have forever been, overwhelmingly white upper-middles.

- Legacy admission ends. Legacy students are those kids accepted into prep schools, colleges, and graduate and professional schools because a grandparent, mother, father, aunt, and/or uncle once attended (and has typically been a solid donor). Some innate and learned candidate qualifications are hoped for and often present in legacies.

Yet, we also know that, historically, those with the wherewithal to be solid donors have tended to be white and don't wonder about their class of origin. Can a legacy student be less than qualified? Ask the first President Bush about Yale and his son. That'll clear it up.

Of course, these schools argue that preferential admissions of these sorts are necessary to the future of the schools and, they'll say, to the general welfare. They may be right, because one can only speculate about the future.

But that's the point.

Affirmative action isn't about what most people assume it's about. Most think it's about the past, about righting wrongs, and about why your kid did or didn't get the admissions deal the kid from across town or across the lawn got.

It isn't.

As with all of the traditional, longstanding admissions preferences, affirmative action is formative; such preferences help define what the professions (and, more broadly, society) will look like in decades and generations. Like all preferences, they're about presumed social good.

The sticking point is the clash between the collective vision of a future where far more people of all origins are modeling for kids what it means to be a good lawyer, doctor, teacher, or CEO and the view of admissions as solely personal. It is personal only as to the thin or thick envelopes, as to the immediacy of elation or pain. Because they help form society's future, admissions are collective in every other way, and, as such, there are vital societal, economic, and cultural interests in some reasonable guarantee of diversity.

Three Thoughts on Near East Antagonism

2010

There will come a time, and that time will arrive sooner than many believe, when Near East Muslims will grasp that Jews—that Israel—is not what holds them back. This is a reason I am (along with every United States president since Mr. Truman) for a two-state solution.

The long-term solution will be about secure borders, mutual respect for Islam's and Judaism's historical and holy sites, formal political recognition of Israel by Palestinians, and other issues yet to be negotiated.

But it will also be about core cultural and regional issues that Israel cannot influence. With a state to manage, Palestinians will be accountable to more than rhetoric, missiles, bullets, and bombs. They, and the nations who support them, will need to come to terms with some stubborn and uncomfortable problems, none of which can be laid at Israel's door.

Ask yourself: Were Israel to be gone in the morning, would poor, Near East Muslims—including Palestinians—genuinely enjoy a new dawn?

I offer three points for your consideration:

I

Religious ideology (any religious ideology) that rejects modernity cannot hope to raise educational standards enough to be competitive and raise living standards for millions. Israel has nothing to do with the grip of medievalism that has retarded much of the Muslim world's economic development. The irony is that it was not always so in the Near East Muslim world: It was a leader in math, the sciences, engineering, architecture, and other forms of design until about four hundred years ago, when it began to become increasingly reactionary, if not xenophobic, finding it more and more difficult to live with and near non-Muslims.

II

No nation—ours, Israel—is without ugly, dismissive, class-based prejudice. Yet, what has to be confronted by poorer Near East Muslims is the back of the hand that wealthy, authoritarian Arab states have continually given to their far poorer regional coreligionists, as evidenced by the many decades of extraordinary and continuing economic disparity between the oil-rich Muslim states and Near East Muslim communities that have not benefited from oil. As far as I can see, nothing external has prevented the geologically fortunate and therefore far more economically robust Islamic states from helping to raise living standards in their much poorer, politically and religiously allied nations and communities. Certainly, Israel has not stopped them.

In part, of course, it's been simpler and more useful for the wealthy autocracies to keep the poor ones impoverished in order to use them as a thorn in Israel's side, as ready cannon fodder. It's been easier to point to Israel as the reason the poor countries and communities live as they do. With a concerted effort, the oil states could, if they genuinely cared about Palestinians, raise living and educational standards within a generation. That they fail to do it, I think, has more to do with class and prejudice against the Jews than with Israel's existence or behavior.

147

III.

Any culture choosing to suppress half its population—women—cannot expect more than a halting development.

I am reminded of the 2011 Saudi imprisonment of 32-year-old Manal al-Sharif for organizing a protest during which she drove a car. Driving a car is, for women, illegal in the kingdom. So are voting, operating a business, and working without a husband's or father's permission.

Ms. al-Sharif's real crime, though, goes beyond the stick shift. An Internet technologies specialist with oil giant Aramco, she organized her protest on Facebook and Twitter, garnering the names of over 600 men and women who saw the rule for what it is: an absurd shackle not only cuffing women but any nation that would so easily embed female infantilization in religion. In a nation where your name on a petition can swiftly have you disappeared, the 600-plus are to be commended. Initially, Ms. al-Sharif and her brother were both arrested and detained. He was sent home with a warning; she was imprisoned.

The routine suppression of women under law is never an avenue toward long-term societal success. This is true no matter how much oil (or whatever resources) you may have, no matter what your religious beliefs. Certainly not all Near East nations deny women the right to drive a car. In how many, though, may they vote? In how many may they work outside the home without a man's permission? In those countries where women are more independent, general living standards improve.

So while Israel is far from perfect (as all Israelis and American Jews know), it remains important to see and only honest to acknowledge that nothing Israel has done or is doing has led to the longstanding choice in the Muslim Near East to regard women as children, nor to that choice's many consequences.

On My 48ᵗʰ Grade School Class Reunion

1963 - 2011

This may be all I know:
Everyone we ever knew when we were twelve
is now a better person, more wonderfully dreadfully
human, for by now, every single one of us has suffered.

Some of us suffered early;
childhood diseases,
intractable private conditions,
incalculable family tragedies;
the scarrings leave imprints on the young who suffer, and more.

The scarrings just cannot, then, be widely felt, and, even if to a
degree fathomed by one or two friends, can so rarely be articulated.

A joy of reunion with your at once faraway, distant and yet
strangely, most intensely close, earliest friends, is that you look over
the very same faces and see the work of each of our mortarpestle
lives,
early and late,
ground into the depths of wisdom, seen with our now grown eyes,
eyes we never saw or had no access then to see, the brows, the ·
foreheads and furrowing souls,
feel an aching, acute warmth in a now knowing
smile,

in a hug or a handshake, and in
the timbre of every single voice that says,
however much success and happiness have found us amid the pain
and loss,

the voices and the looks all say:

Yes.
Of course.
We know.
We just know.

Just Saturday night;

already, and forever, I miss you all.

Looking Through Keyholes: How I Betray the Social Contract Each Day

2011

(Originally published in slightly different form in *Talking Writing*)

I am a writing irony: I continually betray what I'd thought was my rational, robust commitment to the idea of privacy.

I cannot look at you squarely and say that what I write (and what I know that I will write) will honor my old standard of jealously guarding my privacy. I betray privacy, breach it, nearly every day.

Our culture once fiercely prized clearly drawn emotional and personal boundaries. We said that such boundaries ought to be strong, if not impregnable. Outside of formal memoir and overtly autobiographical fiction, social commentators such as I were, until quite recently, far more circumspect than I, in fact, have been.

The lines have fast faded. The late Christopher Lasch wrote in his 1977 book on the American family, *Haven in a Heartless World*[1], that we are safer, better able to move in the world psychically intact, when we work hard to maintain a distinction between our public and private lives. We should protect, he said, the refuge we have in our families; even more so, we should protect the refuge we have in the idiosyncratic confines of our thoughts.

---

[1] Christopher Lasch, *Haven in a Heartless World: The Family Besieged* (Basic Books, 1977)

Our social contract for privacy has been, for at least a generation, deteriorating in metastatic rituals of public confessional. Despite myself, I have contributed through my writing to the spread of the new paradigm and to the old contract's collapse.

I find myself in a strange place. Where I used to recoil reflexively at the steady Oprahizing and reality-programmed nature of our lives, I am intrigued—even somewhat stung—by the fact that my writing contributes to it, as does my interaction with the many who read my daily efforts.

I realize that I've approached this with what Lasch surely would tell me is a layman's aping of a therapeutic relationship—revealing myself by inches so that my audiences feel increasingly comfortable doing the same. I haven't done this consciously. I perceived it only after rereading over a thousand posts I published between October 2008 and March 2012, as well as the comments I received on them.

I reviewed the nearly 800 pieces I've posted at *Open Salon* and the 300-plus pieces I've published at the Pal Talk News Network, at *Talking Writing*, at *Does This Make Sense,* and elsewhere.

I was stunned to discover that at least half my pieces reveal personal parts of my life and/or the lives of family members, friends, and former students—information that, knowing myself, I'd never be inclined to betray outside of my writing, not even to some longstanding friends.

I see now that the pretense that I'm writing under the guise of social commentary has enabled me to exercise online any urge to revelation without the consequences of face-to-face unmasking. This unsettling revelation makes me wonder if my writing—our writing, the explosion of writing in these venues—confirms not so much the thinking of Lasch but rather the feminist writer Carol Hanisch's now nearly forty-year-old assertion that the personal is, in fact, political.[2]

I can certainly say that the political, in my writing, has been and is increasingly deeply personal. If that's right, much of me that's out there—and can never be reeled in—owes itself to and reflects feminist models of thought, sensibility, and interaction far more than I'd imagined.

I've found, too, that readers' responses to my work reflect a willingness, if not an eagerness, to comment as much about themselves as about a position I've taken. I sense that the nature of blog posts may make them more likely to invite personal responses than do published pieces in online magazines, even those that invite commentary.

Here's just one example. When I'd had quite enough of the latest round by right-wing presidential candidates of bashing the poor, particularly those requiring the public's assistance, I decided to write (with her enthusiastic nod) of my wife's having received food stamps when she was just out of art school.

"My Wife Was a Filthy Turn-of-Phrase: On the Dole" was published January 19, 2012 on my *Open Salon* blog. (It is also included in this book.) Nearly all of the fifty responses were from those who supported food stamps and, in many cases, had used them themselves. Many commenters also offered opinions about the broader political issues.

Now, it's possible that I am quite alone among (male?) bloggers in having had to reread many hundreds of my pieces in order to understand that my core may not be what I'd thought it to be. I've come to see that how I write, how I use the personal, is gauged to tease out the personal in others.

---

[2] Carol Hanisch, "The Personal is Political," 1969 (first published in *Notes From the Second Year: Women's Liberation,* 1970), http://www.carolhanisch.org/CHwritings/PIP.html

Lasch may have been at least partly right. We now seem to prefer—even if we're not conscious of or deliberate about it—therapeutic models of presentation or, more accurately, models of written interaction derived from therapeutic models.

He would argue, of course, that the new model of exposing all has supplanted more dispassionate models, ones he believed were useful because they preserved more of our privacy. As I read him, he mourns the therapeutic coup.

I remain conflicted, often thinking that reading *others'* revelatory pieces places me where I ought not to be, despite the fact that I've been invited to walk through the door. Other writers' doors feel all too often more like a series of keyholes. Have I legitimate business taking in others' medical, psychological, financial, religious, and relational histories and intimacies?

Yet, it's inescapable: While I find the newer, perhaps feminist-influenced cultural paradigm often alien, I'm in it up to my ears.

On the Nature of Sexuality and a Straight Person's Commitment to Equality

2011

(Originally published in somewhat different form in *Does This Make Sense?*)

I've often wondered why it has seemed so much easier for straight, progressive Americans to embrace the longstanding women's and civil rights movements than the ongoing struggle for full LGBT civil rights.

I don't think the reticence reflects a lack of understanding that expanding civil rights for some expands them for all. I think it has more to do with sexuality itself—how personal and defining our sexuality is and how locked in we (save, in a sense, the truly bisexual) really are.

While I'll never deeply know—as my wife, Tamar, does—how it feels to be a woman in the United States or—as my son, Graham, does—what it means to move about in this country as a black man, I have felt that I understand something of their experiences of gender and race.

I know something of what Tamar felt when male interviewers years back made assumptions about her potential. Long ago, I was asked by a sneering prep school headmaster in an interview what I *as a Jew* thought of the 1981 Israeli bombing of an Iraqi nuclear plant.

And I know something of what my black son felt when we had, years back, our first conversations about his going to a mall in a

155

racially mixed group. Resenting my wary admonitions about safety, Graham recoiled at the very thought of minority mall guards paying outsized attention to him and his black and Latino friends. Later, he recoiled at the actual experience, when some members of his thoroughly integrated group received more hassling than others from minority mall guards.

These instances are among hundreds experienced by Tamar as a woman, by Graham as black.

While I have understood to a small extent the struggles my wife and son live with, I have never come close to a visceral sense of a gay person's struggle. Nothing within me has ever whispered what same-sex attraction feels like, nor what it feels like to be despised, to be run over rough shod and perhaps ground down, to struggle to overcome the prejudice, and, perhaps, win...for the right to express my sexual love for someone of the same gender.

I wonder how muted, how limited this has made my voice.

My son argues I've no clue what it's like to grow up black here, and he's right. Still, I see his and Tamar's knowledge of the challenges of black people and women in this race-and-gender-crazed land as at least somewhat accessible, gut sensible, a distant cousin in feeling, perhaps, to the challenges Jews and other minorities have faced, that I myself have encountered as a Jew.

The struggles of women and black people have been mainstream dialogue for nearly as long as I've been alive. The movement for LGBT rights is more recent, but it is still the emblematic civil rights movement of the current era. You'd think we'd all have committed to it by now.

I wonder if, for me, it is a kind of visceral leap of faith, one that will always feel different than other struggles for civil rights. Sexuality has primarily been, and perhaps properly, private and personal. Advocating for LGBT rights is about committing to justice in the abstract as well as in the flesh—to addressing sexual issues in front of friends, relatives, and colleagues.

I wonder if—given the nature of our odd, Puritanical culture—this commitment has presented, and presents still, more of a gulf-bridging challenge than advocating for gender and racial rights.

If so, this commitment must be about seeing and believing in what abstract justice and a working democracy requires of us beyond anything we might grasp in our guts, what it demands of us, whether or not we can ever feel—even a little, in our innermost, deeply personal sexual selves—precisely what our dauntless, so very courageous, LBGT colleagues are striving for in this brilliant struggle.

The Al Qaeda Emergency New Leadership Qualifying Questionnaire

2011

(Originally published in *A World of Progress*)

M *ay 2011: Al Qaeda announces that its search for a new leader is underway*

1. Your name:

2. Your courier's name:

3. Your disaffected preteen jihad-in-training (JIT) name:

4. Your Facebook name:

5. Your My-Jihad name:

6. Check all that apply:

___a. I can build a Kalishnikov rifle from sand.

___b. I can wield the Scimitar of the Just Martyr.

___c. If selected, I will give up:

158

____my Comcast account

____my *Sports Illustrated* subscription

____Chinese take-out

____d. I dislike the Renaissance.

____e. I very much disdain modernism.

____f. I simply cannot abide post-modernism.

____g. Jews like d, e, f: I dislike Jews immensely.

____h. I think the Indiana Jones scene where he offs the Brother in the robe who's wielding a scimitar is (check all that apply):

____unfair

____very unfair

____a grossly unfair byproduct of American arrogance

____Hollywood is controlled by Jews

____so is Bollywood

____was plagiarized from an Israeli Army training video

____i. I used to like my Crickett Phone but now I hate what the data package includes.

____j. I think The Temptations were better than the Four Tops.

___k. I am a deeply spiritual killer who refuses to do the Mashed Potato or the Watusi because (check all that apply):

___the singers were female girls

___the records were produced in Jew York

___l. Is there a song in your heart?

___Yes!

___m. I most identify with (check one):

___ Bet you're wondering how I knew

    Of your plans to make me blue

    With some other guy you knew before

    Between the two of us guys

    You know I love you more[1]

___ I don't like you, but I love you,

    Seems that I'm always thinking of you.

    Oh, oh, oh you treat me badly,

    I love you madly,

---

[1] "I Heard It Through the Grapevine," Norman Whitfield and Barrett Strong, 1966.

You really got a hold on me.[2]

____ The night we met I knew I needed you so,

And, if I had the chance, I knew I'd never

Let you go.

So, won't you say you love me?

I'll make you so proud of me![3]

____m. I dislike nosy neighbors with multiple antennae.

____n. I think Pakistani garrison towns aren't really all that.

____o. I think Matlock's Jihad name when he was in the Atlanta Cell should remain among the Pure and never be said aloud: Opie.

____p. I have no fear of:

____ *"24"* reruns

____Penelope Garcia and the *Criminal Minds* profilers

____Abby from *NCIS* or that nerdguy she works with

____Jinns or Djinns

---

[2] "You've Really Got a Hold on Me," Smokey Robinson, 1962.
[3] "Be My Baby," Jeff Barry, Ellie Greenwich, and Phil Spector, 1963.

___q. I can see Ramallah from my house.

Penis Ennui: Why Hebrews Circumcised, Why Some Would Ban It

1972 - 2011

(Originally published in *Does This Make Sense?*)

I am the only person I know to have fainted at a *brit milah*, the ceremonial religious cutting of an eight-day-old Jewish boy's foreskin. I was among colleagues from Akiba Hebrew Academy just west of Philadelphia, at the home of my friend Rabbi Steve Stroiman and his wife, Lucy. We were standing, facing living room windows on a very bright and crisp fall morning in the mid-1970s. Their newborn, Danny, was held high in one hand by the *mohel* as he, Steve, and Lucy chanted a prayer. As the *mohel* raised his other hand, his knife glinting in the sunlight, I went down. Only the grace of another guest, who swiftly moved a folding chair beneath me, prevented me from smacking my bottom onto the floor. She tells me she patted my cheeks and gave me a little brandy to bring me around.

In May 2011, I wrote a piece where I shared my hope that Congress would pass the proposed Girls Protection Act to make it harder for families to spirit girls living here to some overseas destinations to perform genital mutilation in accordance with ancient custom. It now appears that there's an equally strong, if as yet localized, push to outlaw ritual and non-ritual male circumcision. Activists in the movement—they call themselves "intactivists"—argue that regardless of religious or cultural dictates, the practice is nothing more than genital mutilation and must be banned.

According to a June 2011 *New York Times* article by Jennifer Medina[8], a group in San Francisco has already garnered 7,100 signatures in support of the ban, more than the number required to get the issue to ballot in November 2012. Santa Monica is considering a similar move. The measure would "make it illegal to snip the foreskin of a minor within city limits," criminalizing a common practice—and not only among Jews and Muslims, for whom the ritual is sacred. The author of the two proposed bills, Matthew Hess of San Diego, says he intends to push his proposals well beyond his home state.

Ms. Medina notes that the movement has alarmed the Jewish community throughout the country. The concern among Jews is that circumcision has often been intertwined with religious bigotry. In ancient times, circumcision was banned; in the twentieth century, it was used to identify and remove Jews from the general population by both the Russian czar's armies and, more recently, by Hitler's S.S.

The article further notes that circumcision is now performed on between 30 and 50 percent of male babies in the United States; most medical groups take no position on the practice, except to agree that there is no evidence of harm as a general rule.

If a ban were approved in either or both cities, the Supreme Court would likely be called upon to weigh in on the political, religious, legal, and social (not to mention philosophical and medical) complexities that the issue presents. This would not be the Court's first foray into ruling whether religious practices may be socially unacceptable. The Supreme Court tackled the issue of polygamy in 1878 in *Reynolds v. United States*[2]. In its decision, the Court noted that not every action stemming from religious beliefs qualified for First Amendment protection. To make its case, it used as an example

---

[8] Jennifer Medina, "Efforts to Ban Circumcision Gain Traction in California," New York Times, June 4, 2011.
[2] http://law2.umkc.edu/faculty/projects/ftrials/conlaw/reynoldsvus.html

the possibility of human sacrifice: However sincere were the beliefs of the practitioners, the practice clearly would subvert public order.

Mr. Hess and his supporters argue that the ruling applies to circumcision: Society must see it as harmful both to the social order and to millions of individual boys, much as we view female genital mutilation. His motivations may be more complicated, however; he is the publisher of *Foreskin Man,* an online comic book featuring a superhero who does battle with a variety of visual Orthodox-looking stereotypes that the American Anti-Defamation League has denounced as "grotesque anti-Semitic imagery."[3]

Regardless of whether bias is involved, I don't hold with a ban on circumcision, although my reasons might surprise you.

Female genital mutilation and male circumcision are fundamentally different, not only because one has been shown to have many ill effects on the lives of girls and women, and the other has never been shown to be harmful to boys and men. The fact is that female genital mutilation appears to be, everywhere it occurs, not a matter of any religious commitment but a cultural practice designed to keep women subservient. Nowhere do its practitioners make even a pretense of religious compulsion. And that matters to me, because while I am not religious myself, I do give more respect to a practice—particularly a harmless one—if it is done to honor precepts more enduring and honorable than "this is the way we've always done it."

Moreover, for many years I have wondered why my ancient Hebrew clans chose *brit milah* as the definitive sign of attachment to and loyalty to the One. There shouldn't have been a need for any physical mark to distinguish Hebrews from all the other nations competing for land and power in the ancient Near East. But what

---

[3] "ADL Says Anti-Circumcision Comic Book Offends with 'Grotesque' Anti-Semitic Imagery," ADL press release, June 3, 2011.

many Hebrews believed (and many Jews today believe) was that circumcision was a divine edict, ordered in order to signify a special bond.

Why the male? My theory: to tame him.

Before, say, 9,000 to 11,000 years ago, worship seemed to center on the earth goddess. The act of carrying a child and giving birth was seen as supremely powerful: creation itself, replicating over and again everything that is. Women possessed fecundity, an awesome force, perhaps the most regularly occurring awesome force known. Earth goddesses, we know, were often depicted as pregnant.

Gradually, men became aware of their role in creating new life. A shift in power occurred. Men were larger and possessed superior strength, particularly in numbers. They began to worship male gods like Zeus, all-powerful, controlling of even their goddesses, and certainly capable of great violence. The new order was male; it was about strength and force and subjugation.

I propose that the ritual of circumcision was a symbolic check on male power, the first known acknowledgement by men that there is a presence more powerful than male group power. Circumcision would have thus become a foundational admission by men that their own very potent force must be sublimated to a higher truth in order for society to be just.

This is hardly, of course, to suggest that the Hebrew clans always acted justly (or that their descendants always behave justly today). It is to say that the ancient Hebrew clans separated themselves from other ancient Near East tribes by announcing through *brit milah* that unbridled male power never can result in a just world, and that only in living by a code not considered wholly made by men could justice flourish and endure.

Note: Since this essay was originally published, the courts and the voters have rejected the bans in California.

For My Late Father, On Veterans' Day
2011

My dad, along with tens of thousands of other young G.I.s hunkered down in frozen German forests in December 1944, just prior to the Battle of the Bulge, was sent desert boots by mistake. The boots intended for them—the warm ones, the sturdy ones—were sent to North Africa.

The error resulted in trench foot, just short of gangrene. And a good thing, too, because the Nazis overran my dad's syncopatingly-numb-and-exquisitely-pain-riddled position not more than half a month after he and the others with barely any feeling in their feet had been evacuated.

Trench foot spared his life and gave me mine.

In England, the story continues, German POWs were assigned to carry injured Americans on cots onto transport ships bound for Boston and its hospitals. One such German, reading my dad's name on a cot tag, smacked one of my dad's aching, bulbous, and discolored feet as hard as he could. "*Juden*," he spat. My dad saw stars and gritted his teeth, trying hard not to allow the Nazi any pleasure.

Dad recuperated and returned home to Philadelphia, and all his life his nearly hairless feet and calves weren't quite right. He was a lucky, grateful man to the last.

Dad never had a sense that he was a victim of the Germans, of history, of anything. He served proudly in the effort to deny Nazis victory. He knew that the nearly half a million American deaths were necessary and meaningful, however regrettable.

In my career as a teacher, I became aware of what time and distance do to the young people who neither lived through that war nor grew up in the homes of former soldiers. Many of my students—most of them bright, private school children—had no real sense that the Allies were losing the war for four of its five years. They knew the war lasted from September 1939 through early August 1945, but their emotional sense (until I got hold of them) was that Pearl Harbor was very bad but somehow, soon after, we turned it around and won. Maybe that's what winning does to future generations. It's sad, because it minimizes the boys sent home with trench foot from the German front. And the ones blown to bits at Iwo Jima.

To my dad and to all who served, including the numbers of American World War II G.I.s who die now each day, I want to say "Thank you," however inadequate those thanks may be. I'm grateful to you, Dad, and to all of your comrades who served in that war, those you knew and those you never knew, those who died and those who lived, so that we could be here to protect what you saved.

Witness: With His Companions
After the Crucifixion

2012

I'd love to have known, to have witnessed, any number of people, places, events throughout history.

I'd love to have been with King David when, it's said, he had transient possession of God's (and Indy's) Ark.

I'd feel privileged to have had a safe Gettysburg perch those first three days of July 1863 and then to have been at General Lee's side when, after Pickett's miserably failed "charge," he had to tear up his never-delivered note to Lincoln suing the president for peace on terms favorable, of course, to the slaveholders.

I'd be honored to have been at the foot of Sinai among the 600,000 who (we're taught) witnessed the Decalogue descending like a delicate newborn in the arms of Moses.

It would be a treasure to have watched the Allies land in June 1944 on the northern French coast—and to have witnessed the eyes of the Nazi lookouts pop as our massive invasion armada emerged from the thick, predawn mist.

I'd like to have been in that 1974 arena in Kinshasa to see Muhammad Ali fight George Foreman, the Supreme Court having overturned in 1971 Ali's ludicrous draft-evasion conviction. I'd like to have been a 23-year-old watching him, cheering him, as he regained his championship title, a title that ought never have been stripped.

I'd trade a great deal to have been, at age 12, at the steps of the Lincoln Memorial on a late August afternoon to hear Martin Luther King proclaim, "In the words of the old Negro spiritual, 'Free at last, free at last, thank God Almighty we are free at last!'"

There are hundreds, if not thousands, such moments for which I hunger.

But most of all, I'd want to be among the closest companions of that ancient, protean, mesmerizing rabbi Jesus in the three years of his public, itinerant teaching prior to his murder at Jerusalem and in the two decades after those companions fled upon news of his arrest and execution.

Of the four canonized narrative gospels—Mark, Matthew, Luke, and John—and the two dozen additional gospels known to scholars and the Church—the Sayings Gospels, the Infancy Gospels, the gospels of Peter, Mary, and Thomas, Paul's often magnificently composed letters, and the rest—there exists a stunning two-decade chasm, a total blackout, between the crucifixion, in 33 C.E., and the first writings about Jesus.

We have no written account of how his closest companions got on and what they did in the twenty years after his death.

The earliest gospel, Mark's, was written c. 70 C.E. Even the letters of Paul, Timothy, and James to the fledgling Jesus-believing communities at, say, Corinth, Thessalonica, Ephesus, or Rome date at their earliest to c. 50, twenty or so years after Jesus was so violently cut off from them.

I'd like to know why nothing in writing exists from those earliest years and why some of the oral accounts made it into the gospels and some didn't.

171

Were his close companions emotionally struck mute by the untimely loss of their friend and leader?

Or was no one in that first community sufficiently literate? Most of his Galilean followers were almost certainly unlettered, but *all*, and even at Jerusalem? That's tough to believe.

Or were they controlled enough in the midst of devastating personal loss to understand that, wherever they fled, anything said about Jesus had to be transmitted orally only, for both self and group protection?

This, to me, makes the most sense. This was the Passover Festival, when masses traditionally poured into the city and Roman procurators routinely ordered peasant irritants killed. After all, in the half-century after Jesus' birth, records suggest Roman agents at Jerusalem crucified over 50,000 in Judea—southern Israel—alone. That's an average of just under 20 crucifixions per week.

So, as devoted to their friend as his disciples were, could they have possibly imagined that Romans saw Jesus as they themselves had seen him? For them to have believed Roman authority saw Jesus as a holy man would not have been an expression of devotion. It would have been one of lunacy—a refutation of everything every Jewish peasant of that place and time knew about the tools of routinely brutal Greek and then Roman colonial oppression.

By the late 50s, we have abundant written evidence that Paul and his companions are organizing home-based churches in communities throughout the Mediterranean and in Rome itself and then writing to the parishioners. And 20-some years on from Paul's work, we have Mark writing the first canonical gospel.

I don't want to speculate as to what went on. I want to be there, to light up and penetrate those earliest dark years and to see, to really know, how and why the first Jerusalem community survived its near decimation, its scattering after the murder of its leader, and how it once again coalesced and grew.

172

I want to have known the charisma of the rabbi who was Jesus. I want to have been among the first to hear his words on justice and the Kingdom of God spoken over and over and over again, throughout Galilee and the south—the striking, illuminating parables, stories, and sayings forming a distinctly Jewish paradigm of justice, the basis for all extant gospels.

And then I want my own ears to hear that silence and my eyes to see beneath it, because the story of the companions of Jesus may well be the most unlikely yet overwhelming success story of all unrecorded time.

America's Philosophical and Cultural Chasm, at Its Core

2013

The very name of our country speaks to unity. But, at bottom, our history is more often one of contentious chasms.

An early 2013 series of letters to the *New York Times*[1]—provoked by President Barack Obama's second inaugural address and conservative reaction to it—took a keen look at the continual American tension.

Here's my sense of it.

These schisms invariably have to do with the proper role of federal and state power; if, how, and why we may restrict the use of enormous private sums; how enormous public sums are obtained and spent; and the never-simple role of religion in a nation distinguished by a fundamentally secular Constitution.

The enormous rift that undergirds all these ongoing debates is philosophical and cultural, not simply political and economic. These are the same divisions that sprang to action when the Reconstruction Amendments, women's suffrage, labor organizing rights, Social Security, Medicare, Medicaid, landmark Civil Rights legislation,

---

[1] "An Inaugural for the 21st Century," letters to the *New York Times,* January 22, 2013, http://www.nytimes.com/2013/01/23/opinion/an-inaugural-for-the-21st-century.html

abortion rights, and the right to adequate health care, were fought for and, largely, finally, won.

The American chasm at its core is the gulf between two social perspectives. On one hand, there are those who view society as a collection of individuals essentially and appropriately isolated, who choose to meet only when self-interest, most typically in commerce or defense, make group activity expedient. On the other, we have those of us who see society as informed, a priori, by a series of mutual commitments that require us to regard all of our actions and decisions as impacting both ourselves and (unknown) others.

No recent iteration of this chasm was more starkly revealed than when news came of the extraordinarily myopic initial refusal of hundreds of U.S. House members to allocate funds to the miserable souls barely hanging on in Hurricane Sandy's wake, months after the event.

I am clear in my own obligations: Mutual commitment is the proper approach to leading an ethical American life. The injunctions of my secular upbringing as well as my ethnic/religious culture and the United States Constitution (as well as common sense) tell me that taking care of the destitute, the widow, the orphan, the ill, the elderly, the unsheltered and consistently hungry, in the face of ongoing violent, systemic, and structural inequality, is integral to what it means to be a person and an American citizen. I see it also as my obligation as a Jew.

The words and public acts of the rabbi who was Jesus teach me that he understood the insistence of the prophets. From Moses and Miriam to Deborah, Elijah, Isaiah, Jeremiah, with the same message finding voice through Dr. Martin Luther King, Jr., Harriet Tubman, Sister Simone Campbell, and beyond, this insistence is reflected in a single thought, which I encapsulate as follows:

To be a person, to be a complete person, means seeing the possibilities for and moral necessity of envisioning and then enacting universal justice, here, right here.

175

Their insistence is my steady obligation; it informs my assessment of and response to every policy proposal, regulation, and law. That charge informs the writing and organizing that is my activism. It daily reminds me that I am fully a person only to the extent that I am for the least of us as much as I am for my family and for myself.

Baby, We Were Taught This Way

2011

No one's going to make the claim that California is still the Golden State of America's dreams. That fantasy's long gone. Aside from California's overwhelming fiscal deterioration (it is only now clawing back), the fantasy's end should have been clear by the mid-eighties when films such as the [date of film] classic *River's Edge* grimly (and grimily) detailed the depraved depths of that dream-turned-nightmare. In case Americans weren't yet convinced that things had gone very wrong, 2003 brought the terrifying film *Thirteen,* which dissected the brutal quality of everyday lower-middle-class Southern California culture.

And yet California still has the capacity to surprise us with forward-thinking legislation. In July 2011, Governor Jerry Brown signed a bill requiring all California school districts to teach gay history in social science classes. Ian Lovett wrote in a July 2011 *New York Times* article[1] that the law "mandates that the contributions of gays and lesbians in the state and the country be included in social science instruction and in textbooks." While new textbooks weren't available by the end of the year, supplementary materials were.

The good that this can do, over time, to impart useful knowledge—and even, perhaps, to reduce bullying—remains to be seen. I'd like

---

[1] Ian Lovett, "California to Require Gay History in Schools," *New York Times,* July 14, 2011.

to think that if, a generation hence, there's more respect for all kinds of people in California, it will be partly because Californians can say, to paraphrase Lady Gaga's brilliant, energizing anthem, "Baby, we were taught this way!"

The Civil Rights Mandate of Our Era

2012

An address on LGBT rights given at the U.S. Capitol on April 22, 2012, a day of worldwide marches for equality

First, I wish to say this: We are winning.

We are winning, and we will continue to move from strength to strength and achieve complete victory. We are making this nation a place where all citizens may enjoy equal civil rights under law.

Today, throughout the world, we are holding these marches to raise up the need for thoroughgoing justice for LGBT citizens. Taken together, these events, in well over 30 cities here and overseas, are unique in the history of social justice activism. You are part of a movement that demands justice not only here in Washington, DC, not only in other cities in the United States, but across the globe.

Marchers have gathered in Albany and New York City, New York; Atlanta and Athens, Georgia; Chicago, Illinois; Dayton, Ohio; Memphis, Tennessee; McCallen, Texas; Oklahoma City and Tulsa, Oklahoma; Portland, Oregon; Jacksonville, Florida; New Orleans, Louisiana; Baltimore, Maryland; Las Vegas, Nevada; Salt Lake City, Utah; Jackson, Mississippi; and Marquette, Michigan.

They have gathered in Pakistan; in Port Elizabeth, South Africa; in Bacolod City and Manila in the Philippines; in Great Britain; in Namibia; in Kampala, Uganda; in Abija, Nigeria; and in Tanzania.

This is the reach of your justice movement. We are global.

My name is Jonathan Wolfman. I'm from Maryland, the eighth state to have passed a marriage equality bill. I am also chief editor for political essays of the Internet site *Castle Gay Guide,* just one of thousands of important weapons in this fight. The site has regular visitors from well over 80 nations and a page devoted to LGBT civil rights struggles in parts of the world where you may still, under law, be sentenced to life—or to death—for "breathing while gay." That's no exaggeration.

That some are marching today in several of those nations takes guts and a belief in ultimate justice. I salute all marchers today but especially those who risk arrest and beatings and worse for their commitment.

I am also an administrator of the group that planned these equality marches and rallies.

As a straight ally in this movement, I cannot know what it feels like to be gay, what it means to move in this world as an LGBT citizen. I don't know what it feels like to be black or Hispanic or Native American, either—what it is to navigate this world as a person of color. Nor do I know what facing discrimination as a woman feels like.

Yet, I know for certain what it is to be a Jew in America. I know the challenge it is to live up to the rigors of my ethical traditions, here, in this place. Thoroughgoing legal equality for all citizens, as I read it, is a demand of my tradition. It is a demand of the only true American exceptionalism, the ethical weight of our Bill of Rights, that brief and brilliant document which informs every thought I have about civil rights and liberties. It is an uncompromising demand that all adult citizens enjoy equally the obligations, responsibilities, and rights that our basic law affirms and affords.

I want to ask you a question.

Is there anyone within the sound of my voice who believes we would be a better nation were we to return to a time when states could decide whether or not people of different races could marry one another? The era of those vile antimiscegenation laws—do you know when it ended? Do you know when the Supreme Court finally stripped racist state legislatures of their so-called right to bar blacks and whites from marrying one another? 1967. Just forty-five years ago. In *Loving v. Virginia*, the Court declared every existing antimiscegenation law dead. States did not, it turned out, have the right to enshrine common, crass racial bigotry in law.

I have a second question.

Is there anyone who can make anything close to a reasonable argument as to why states ought to be able to pass laws denying marriage to LGBT citizens? If you believe that you can, you must first—and with clarity, precision, and absolutely no hint of sloganeering—tell us why it is you recoil at laws that prevent states from barring interracial marriage and yet seem content with states asserting a right to so bar adult citizens who are gay.

You must do so not only without appeal to slogan but also without appeal to religious precepts. You must not appeal to your religion not because religious dicta are illegitimate in themselves, but because in our system of laws, they have no place in determining the rights of citizens.

I'd like to focus on marriage equality head-on. I want to address the most common objections to it—seven of them—one at a time.

Briefly, though, I'll first say this: By now, it ought to be clear that—aside from those who cannot distinguish religious law from democratic, civil law and values—those against marriage equality won't consider it for one clear reason. Marriage not only suggests a cultural imprimatur that sidelines religious imperatives in a democracy but, more so, confers power—real economic and social power—in a wide array of everyday situations and nearly every aspect of law, including taxation, inheritance, medicine, child custody, and housing.

At bottom, people who advocate for inequality want to restrict the enormous power marriage grants to people with whom they feel a kinship of sexuality, to people whose sexuality they believe they understand. They recoil from sharing the civil legal power they have with people whose sexual cores they cannot grasp and believe they will never understand.

Yet, that's hardly anything close to a reasonable basis for denying equality.

Inequality mocks our Bill of Rights as well as our Fourteenth Amendment's Equal Protection Clause, whose purposes are, without any question, to protect minority rights over the whims and prejudices of majorities.

There are, as I say, seven common objections to equality. They were, in January 2012, the subject of an editorial, "Don't Tamper with Same-Sex Marriage Law," in the *Concord Monitor*, New Hampshire's leading daily[1]. I applaud the *Monitor* on its progressive vision. Here are their responses but in my words.

1. *Marriage is between one man and one woman.*

This is a declaration—a declaration of bigotry—not an argument. The statement cannot be taken seriously.

2. *Marriage has been restricted to heterosexuals for thousands of years.*

Slavery was an ancient practice, too. So was barring women from participation in politics. People with disabilities were routinely locked away in institutions.

---

[1] *Monitor* staff, "Don't Tamper with Same-Sex Marriage Law," *Concord Monitor,* January 3, 2012.

3. *Marriage is for procreation.*

Often, that's right. Yet infertile straight couples marry every day. Those with no interest in having children marry. We do not force couples past their childbearing years to divorce nor do we bar them from marriage. Having children has never been the sole reason couples marry.

4. *Same-sex couples don't do as good a job raising children.*

There are all sorts of good parents and a wide variety of bad ones. Sexual orientation has nothing to do with it. Nor is there a legislative push to ban other sorts of truly bad parents —child molesters, bank robbers—from marrying. Studies show no benefit to children of heterosexual couples over same-sex couples as to a child's succeeding educationally, living within the law, making close and healthy bonds with peers and elders, nor any other quality-of-life issue. And no study ever has come close to suggesting that children of gay couples have a higher frequency of being gay themselves than emerging adolescents of straight couples.

Being gay is not contagious.

5. *Same-sex marriage will start us down a path toward legalized polygamy and incest.*

Do you see signs of rampant polygamy or incest in your neighborhood? No? Neither do I in mine.

This is a cheap, vapid scare tactic.

If some legislator pushed a law allowing brothers and sisters to marry, say, or a "Dick and Jane May Marry Their Very Good Dog Spot" law, legislatures could just vote "No."

6. *Gay relationships are immoral.*

Some religions preach that. Yet, legislators represent all their constituents, not just those who share their religious beliefs. They must not impose their own religious beliefs on their constituents. My freedom from your religion in our civil law is as critical as your freedom to practice your religion.

7. *Same-sex marriage threatens the institution of marriage.*

This may be the most ludicrous idea going. Encouraging marriage simply encourages marriage. It is impossible to see how the gay marriage next door threatens my straight marriage. It is equally impossible to understand how the legalization of gay marriage could possibly convince straight people not to marry or encourage them to split up.

Do some straight people object to sharing the word "marriage?" Well: tough. These bigots are no different from those who objected to African-Americans sharing the word "citizen."

Last month the New Hampshire legislature held a vote to repeal its two-year-old marriage equality law. Know what happened? Over sixty Republican legislators never made it to the vote—they found better to do that Wednesday afternoon. Even they knew they'd look silly. They chose to absent themselves from the vote and the reversal failed overwhelmingly.

We are winning. Legislators in every state and in Congress now understand that the movement for thoroughgoing LGBT rights is winning—too slowly for sure, yet justice's arc, as Dr. King taught, is unstoppable, however long it may be.

I ask you again: Should we allow states once more to ban marriage between people of different races as they did here until 1967?

Attempts to haul us backwards may succeed temporarily, but they cannot succeed over time.

A last idea: Not all voting is democratic. Voting on the fundamental constitutional rights of adult citizens is not an exercise in democracy. While we must, out of practicality, support legislative and popular efforts to vote, state by state, for equality on same-sex marriage bills, we know that it is offensive and absurd for majorities to vote on the basic legal rights of minorities. The Supreme Court simply must affirm that it is our Constitution and not the whims of the electorate that, in the end, determine rights under law.

We require for LGBT citizens the same rights under law as racial minorities have and—as to marriage—realized once and for all in 1967. The truth is, too, that we straight people do not need to understand the sexuality of others. All we need to know is that, under law, all adult citizens are one.

There really are two kinds of people in the world: cynics and skeptics.

A cynic excuses smug moral isolation because he himself is myopic and inactive and believes that not much good is ever really possible. He rarely, if ever, attempts anything new and challenging regardless of the potential benefit and, in the end, he is boring. More, a cynic is a person who never affects history even when the potential for good and for justice is inside him, and sadly, passively, becomes lost to history. A cynic never wins.

A skeptic tends to think, then act, assuming we are all one in this open boat, tossed on the waves together. Even though she's wary, knowing that good and bad are both always possible, she continually eyes the landscape for new ideas. She is concerned when she cannot test those ideas out, and so she often does, adding to human creation and to justice.

Be a skeptic. You will not be lost to history. Now, go finish this fight and win.

Why I'd Join the NRA

2013

Y ou may have heard of Larry Ward, the Washington, D.C.-based NRA apologist and right-wing marketing master whose stellar idea it was to hold a National Gun Appreciation Day roughly to coincide both with President Obama's second inauguration and with what would have been Martin Luther King's eighty-third birthday.

And that's hardly Mr. Ward's most stellar idea. The man brims over with them.

On a January 2013 CNN panel, Mr. Ward said with a straight face that general gun ownership among black slaves would have been the answer to captivity.[1] Four million slaves, Mr. Ward told an incredulous interviewer, would have been able to free themselves from the brutal rule of plantation owners—if only they'd remembered to amass millions of rifles, handguns, and tens of millions of rounds of ammunition.

Let that one sink in.

And allow me to share with you a suggestion I took from a South

---

[1] Andrew Kirell, "Gun Appreciation Day Leader to CNN: If Blacks Had Guns, They Never Would Have Been Slaves," *Mediaite,* January 11, 2013, http://www.mediaite.com/tv/gun-appreciation-day-leader-to-cnn-if-blacks-had-guns-they-never-would-have-been-slaves/

Carolina caller when I was interviewed on a radio show[2] about my gun-related writing. Eric Smith (he's pleased for me to name him here) suggested that the NRA should ditch its American eagle-with-the-rifle-in-its-beak logo. In line with the NRA's and Mr. Ward's concern for blacks who forgot to arm themselves while they were slaves, Mr. Smith suggests a replacement logo for the organization—a portrait, actually. A portrait of Nat Turner.

Mr. Turner, a slave in Southhampton County, Virginia, for all of his thirty years, did remember he needed firearms, and this emboldened him to become the architect of the most successful slave rebellion in the antebellum period. In August 1831, between fifty and sixty Virginia slaveholders were killed, as were, of course, over fifty rebelling black men. Many, many hundreds more—most of whom had not participated in the uprising—were beaten regularly for the rest of their shortened lives. For slaveholders, it turned out, were not inclined to look favorably on black men with guns. Nat Turner, of course, was executed.

Within weeks after the three-day rebellion was put down, Virgina, along with other Southern states, passed laws making the education of slaves or free black people a criminal act. New laws also restricted the right of blacks to assemble on the streets, even peaceably. In Virginia, white ministers were required to be present at black worship services.

Mr. Smith's suggestion leads me to ask a question of Mr. Wade and the NRA: If you would have been concerned enough to try to help alleviate the plight of the Nat Turners and John Browns and the 4,000,000 antebellum blacks who forgot to arm themselves, shouldn't you also consider updating your concern by hanging on your office wall—pictures of Russell Means of the American Indian Movement and Black Panthers Huey Newton and Eldridge Cleaver?

---

[2] "Inside Politics with David Calef," WOIC Radio, Columbia, South Carolina, January 12, 2013.

Heck. If you do, *I'll* sign up....

For My Son, a Champion Marksman

2012

I've never owned a gun. I've never even fired one. I've little interest in weaponry.

My 23-year-old son, on the other hand, is a champion marksman who has owned his gun, an FNP-45, for years. He's a wise, sober gun owner. He faithfully cares for it and for the safety of himself, his parents, and his friends. He's thoroughly uninterested in owning an assault weapon, and he seems satisfied with his one pistol and one rifle, which he uses for hunting and long-range target shooting.

He and I largely agree as to what firearms laws ought to look like and have a lively, ongoing dialogue about personal, political, economic, and cultural issues related to firearms ownership. One such conversation was on a map from a December 2012 *Washington Post* column by Ezra Klein[1].

The map correlates the number of firearm deaths to gun-control restrictions in the United States, state by state. While the map was created in 2007, I doubt that it would look significantly different today. It's evident that having more guns in the hands of citizens does not—contrary to well-crafted myths by lobbyers and manufacturers—create safer environments.

---

[1] Ezra Klein, "Twelve Facts about Guns and Mass Shootings in the United States," *Washington Post Wonkblog,* December 14, 2012, http://www.washingtonpost.com/blogs/wonkblog/wp/2012/12/14/nine-facts-about-guns-and-mass-shootings-in-the-united-states/

The fact is that the more guns that are held by a state's private citizens and the fewer regulations that are put in place to protect children, the more gun-related deaths a state has. Louisiana, for example, has many more firearms-related deaths per capita than other states, and it also has among the least restrictive gun codes.

I would never support restrictions that would deny my son the joy marksmanship brings him and the skills he increasingly hones. Yet, he and I both recognize the sickening chasm between his joy and skill and the suffering loose regulation brings. My son and I agree that federal law must now—and for good—address that awful chasm.

The Church Should Not Ditch Its Pedophiles

2012

My hometown, Philadelphia, became known over the past decade for its criminally accused and criminally liable priests, 37 of them. One of them, Monsignor William Lynn—the first member of the U.S. Catholic Church hierarchy to suffer a conviction in the scandal—is serving a serious prison term not for rape but for helping to bury the pedophilia scandal by shredding internal Church documents. Copies were subsequently found (by my guess, saved by some heroic female office lay worker in the Archdiocese).

The Archdiocese is also now known for the fact that, in Philadelphia, the Church has not lived up to its no-tolerance pledge. Like many mammoth institutions, the Church has found advancing molesters onward and, at times, upward, far simpler than confrontation. In some cases, the Church simply removed these men from the priesthood.

I am not in favor of the Church simply ridding itself of these priests. If that's zero tolerance, it's flawed. The Church should be held accountable to its faithful and to the rest of us—including those who have taught distraught teens after their horrified parents have pulled them from diocesan schools—by taking full responsibility for these men. The Church recruited, groomed, educated, trained, and ordained them and provided them, worldwide and for generations, extraordinary access to tens of millions of children.

Cashiering these men would force secular society to wholly assume a responsibility that is not wholly ours. There's no reason to think that pedophilic priests, defrocked and loosed onto the streets, would be less dangerous than they were, say, at Saint Paul's or Saint Bart's. In fact, defrocked and on the loose, they would be harder to identify within the thousands of communities their presence would make vulnerable.

Unless civil society is prepared swiftly to try, convict, and imprison these men—all of them and for decades—the Church should not be permitted to foist pederasts, one after the next, on the rest of us. Zero tolerance should mean that the Church, in an oversight arrangement with secular criminal authority, pays for their upkeep and keeps them in positions and locations that never allow them to associate with anyone under 21. That's not as much of a stretch as it may seem. States attorneys have, in fact, considered using RICO (Racketeer Influenced and Corrupt Organizations) statutes to go after malignant dioceses.

While the Church has become a far-too-safe haven for the sexually and emotionally compromised, it has shown itself too many times to be unwilling, on its own, to keep these priests cloistered for the balance of their lives and thus unable to perpetrate further harm.

I hope that the new pope, Francis, has the fortitude to begin to turn this about.

Women's Health Care and Genuine Religious Freedom

2012

The U.S. Conference of Catholic Bishops and lay Catholics throughout the business community have ramped up their intrusions into secular law and life by claiming, in lobbying efforts and in court, that the Affordable Care Act corrodes religious liberty.

Their specific target has been the ACA's requirement that all employers provide contraceptive coverage in their health plans, even those employers who are affiliated with religious institutions or whose religious beliefs forbid the use of contraceptives.

A strong and smart blow for freedom was recently struck by federal judge Carol Jackson in St. Louis in *O'Brien v. HHS.*[1] (Ironically, President George H.W. Bush appointed Judge Jackson.)

Judge Jackson noted that while the Affordable Care Act exempts churches, mosques, and other houses of worship from the contraception coverage requirement, it does not and ought not exempt owners of secular businesses. In the case she threw out, a Missouri mining company owner had sued the federal Department of Health and Human Services in order to be able to deny contraceptive coverage based on his private religious beliefs. Judge Jackson made clear that a for-profit, secular company can't qualify

---

[1] http://docs.justia.com/cases/federal/district-courts/missouri/moedce/4:2012cv00476/119215/50/0.pdf?1348931108

for a religious exemption simply on the basis of the owner's private beliefs.

Judge Jackson ruled, too, that the First Amendment's guarantee of religious freedom does not exempt secular individuals or entities—such as businesses—from adhering to the law, even when a person's specific belief is sincere. And, needless to say, even if the mining company's owner is sincere, exempting him or his business from the law would invite all sorts of insincere business owners to deny contraception coverage simply to save money at the expense of women employees.

There are many similar ACA-related cases now being heard throughout the country. My hope is that Judge Jackson's decision is seen precisely for what it is: a clear and bold defense not only for the rights of women but, by drawing clear lines between church and state, for religious freedom.

And Jesus Hopped on the Nuns' Bus

2012

The Vatican has viciously gone after American nuns of late for, as Rome sees it, their hyperfocus on the poor and outspoken positions on the Republican budget proposals, health reform, women's health issues, and general economic reform. It reminds me that a few serious scholars conducting historical research on Jesus have more than once wondered—above a whisper—whether, chronologically, the first of the four canonical gospels, Mark's, could have been composed by a woman.

In brief, the scene in which an unnamed woman places costly perfume on Jesus' head as he visits a Bethany household struck by leprosy[1] is thought, by some historians, to be a possible signature— Mark's anonymous signature.

By this thinking, the unnamed woman herself may well be Mark. If this were proven to be so, it would be significant not simply because of the misogynous history it would challenge but because of what Jesus says specifically of her.

When, in the story, the men at the scene admonish her for presuming such closeness, Jesus upbraids them, telling them, in effect, that only she intuitively understands that his body may well shortly be in need of some perfume.

In other words, only a woman—this woman—fully understands the risks Jesus has assumed through three years of increasingly strident

---

[1] Mark 14: 3-9.

195

antipoverty agitation and repeated symbolic performances aimed at underscoring and uplifting the message of a justice-demanding God.

In historian and former priest John Dominic Crossan's *The Last Week*[2], he and fellow historian Marcus Borg suggest that, whether or not anyone could ever really show that Mark was a woman, for the woman in *this* scene, "Easter came early that year." That is, she seems to thoroughly understand the man's program and not only what it will surely cost him but also that it will survive his death, rise, and live on.

Further, Crossan surmises, Mark has Jesus tell his audience what none of his male companions seem to understand: their friend is certainly going to die, and pretty soon, and for the sake of the God of Justice.

The scene ends, most remarkably, with Jesus telling the men that when the stories of his work spread after he's gone, they will be told "in memory of her," that is, in her honor, *not* theirs.

Is there a more symbolic and fundamental ennobling of marginalized women in all of our common religious literature? In ancient Near East cultures, poor women were barely regarded as persons, let alone as people to remember, to honor. Could this vignette be Mark's signature?

No proof will likely be found either way. The earliest copies of *Mark,* which was declared part of the official canon in 325 C.E. at Nicaea, made no mention of whether the unnamed woman had ever been known or written of further.

What I do know is that some of the American nuns who have objected strenuously to the new (male) oversight of their work undertook a nine-state bus tour in June 2012 under the leadership of

---

[2] Marcus J. Borg and John Dominic Crossan, *The Last Week: A Day-by-Day Account of Jesus's Final Week in Jerusalem* (HarperOne, 2006).

Sister Simone Campbell. As they began their trip, an Associated Press piece described the aims of the Nuns On The Bus Tour as they began their trip:

> "A group of Roman Catholic nuns began a nine-state bus tour protesting proposed federal budget cuts Monday, saying they weren't trying to flout recent Vatican criticisms of socially active nuns but felt called to show how Republican policies are affecting low-income families.

> "The tour was organized by Network, a Washington-based Catholic social justice group criticized in a recent Vatican report that said some organizations led by nuns have focused too much on economic injustice while failing to promote the church's teachings on abortion and same-sex marriage. The Vatican asked U.S. bishops to look at Network's ties to another group of nuns it is reorganizing because of what the church calls 'serious doctrinal problems.'

> "Sister Simone Campbell, Network's executive director, while the tour may appear to have been organized to counter recent criticism of social activist nuns by the Vatican and American bishops, it was not. The timing was in response to consideration of the federal budget in Congress, she said."[3]

I know who's traveling with those women; that rabbi hopped this bus long since.

---

[3] David Pitt, "Nuns Start Tour Protesting Republican Budget Plan," Associated Press, June 18, 2012.

197

And Jesus Stopped at Providence

2012

My interest in historical-Jesus research has deeply Jewish roots.

I'm convinced, based largely on my reading of Professor John Dominic Crossan's writings and those of his colleagues in the Jesus Seminar of the Westar Institute, that Jesus' public life and personal sacrifice was one long, repetitive, creative, and exquisitely painful and beautiful protest—almost performance art—against the collusion of Jewish religious authorities with the systemic Roman oppression of the Jewish homeland and, particularly, of its destitute citizens.

Authentic Jewish authority—the Torah—demands that our poorest—our widows, our waifs, our landless, our ill, our infirm—be cared for by the very social structures and legal authorities that, far too easily in Jesus' day, cooperated with the inauthentic authority of the Roman occupation. Rome's rapidly dislocating, impoverishing, utterly destructive urbanization and military and economic rape of the homeland given to the Hebrew clans by God was an abiding, escalating outrage, wholly inconsistent with that of God's abiding demand for justice.

Despite the fact that Jesus never stood trial before the Jewish High Priest, or Pilate, we know what his performances got him in his likely one and only sojourn to Jerusalem—crucified, as were thousands of others. It is, however, not too much to say that glimpses of the man and his art may, even now, be seen.

You've caught many of those glimpses, at food banks, at clothing donation centers, inside women's shelters, marching beside Gandhi, Dr. King, and the nameless thousands and their millions of

198

supporters last year at Oakland, at Wall Street, and elsewhere. Had you been in Providence, Rhode Island, in September 2012, you might have caught another glimpse—a tiny yet very powerful one—of the ongoing performance for justice.

It's a small and unusual action and perhaps one that won't be seen elsewhere or, at least, not for a long while. Yet, it could be replicated; it could spread.

On September 11, 2012, the state legislature at Providence passed the nation's—perhaps the world's—first law on behalf of the homeless. The Rhode Island Homeless Bill of Rights guarantees that those destitute and living on the streets may, unmolested by police and businesses, use public buildings, sidewalks, parks, and transportation "without discrimination on the basis of his or her housing status" and guarantees a "reasonable expectation of privacy" as to personal belongings.

This is to say, Rhode Island has established a statewide personhood of the destitute under law—an uplifting, creative law, striking at the bleak heart of the continuing American war on the poor. Two millennia late for the ancient rabbi, yes, and in only one state, yet I'm betting the rabbi's giving Little Rhody a Standing-O, applauding and nodding, his grin very broad.

Cowards: The Senate Rejects the U.N. Treaty on Disabilities

1955 - 1990 - 2012

While I wore rather ungainly leg braces pretty much from the time I could walk through first grade, I don't recall needing unusual accommodations at school or elsewhere. In any case, none would have been available at my mid-1950s affluent suburban grade school even if I had needed them.

My delight in the passage of the Americans with Disabilities Act in 1990 may have resonated back to childhood sensibilities, yet the reason I most welcomed the ADA was that I had by then spent years teaching and serving as an administrator at public and independent schools where children with all sorts of disabilities struggled at the whims of boards of directors and local school committees that rarely saw as worthwhile dedicated expenditures for special needs kids.

Even after President Bush signed the legislation, thousands of county boards and private school directors were reluctant to make necessary changes. They seldom thought, say, putting in ramps (let alone elevators) made sense, even when the federal government was footing much of the cost. Yet, over time, throughout America (and with federal funding for all sorts of local initiatives at stake) the accommodations were made and lives were bettered.

The ADA's reach, of course, extends beyond schools to every kind of public access and accommodation imaginable, and justly so. Our law was seen as a global model, serving as a standard. Until December 4, 2012.

On that day, the United States Senate made a self-absorbed ass of itself, voting down a move to join the United Nations Convention on the Rights of Persons with Disabilities, a treaty based entirely on its own 1990 legislation. The treaty's sole obligation for ratifying nations would be to do precisely what the ADA enjoins the United States to do: "ban discrimination against persons with disabilities."

And yet, by a vote of 61 against to 38 in favor of joining the treaty, the Senate rejected ratification. All Democrats voted to join the treaty. Republicans voting for the treaty included John McCain (AZ), Kelly Ayotte (NH), John Barrasso (WY), Scott Brown (MA), Susan Collins (ME), Olympia Snowe (ME), Richard Lugar (IN), and Lisa Murkowski (AK). Some Republicans, even a few who had cosponsored the legislation, voted, in the end, against it, for fear that, in two years, they'd lose in primary fights with the far right (as Indiana's Mr. Lugar did in the spring of 2012).

At 89 and ailing, former Republican presidential candidate and longtime Senate Majority Leader Bob Dole (KS) attended the floor debate a week after undergoing serious medical procedures at Walter Reed Military Medical Center. His Republican colleagues ignored his quiet pleas for passage.

While the treaty will come up again for a vote, it's clear that many senators remain in thrall to the post-Cold War far right, a self-referencing reactionary movement that sees any act that is in accordance with the United Nations, *any act*, as a serious, potentially crippling loss of our national sovereignty. Never mind that the treaty asks no nation to sublimate its laws to international rules. Never mind that the treaty asks only that all nations to act toward disabled citizens as we ourselves have had to behave, under our own laws, for nearly a generation.

Although these cowardly zealots are unlikely to feel ashamed, they need to be at least defeated the next time the treaty is up for debate. They need, as well, to be bounced from our Senate.

Justice for the Children at Newtown

2012

Nothing exists of itself alone—not in art, not in politics, not in economics, not in science, not in love, not in law, not in hate, not in violence, not in justice.

In the world of hate, events never simmer or boil over alone. Eruptions come fast upon one another: a viral, syncopating feeding. We'd note that throbbing, were the eyes of our days wide enough, had we more time to see this and much more:

- In 1963, well over fifty violent assaults or murders of black people occurred in Birmingham in the month prior to the Klan killings of four black girls in a church basement.

- In 1994, the year before the Oklahoma City bombing, hundreds of small acts of right-wing terror were recorded at FBI bureaus throughout the Southwest.

- In 1998, in Laramie, Wyoming, young Matthew Shepard was murdered because he was gay. He became the face of a generation of activist effort in a way not dissimilar to how Emmet Till became the face of the nascent modern civil rights movement in the mid- 1950s. Mr. Till, visiting Mississippi from the more liberal North, was murdered for whistling at a white woman.

- And in 2010, in Hungary, the extreme right-wing, openly anti-Semitic party, Jobbik, garnered just under a sixth of the votes in parliamentary elections, up from well under one percent in the 2006 election. This would not have surprised people who know Hungary's modern history, as it has a sad place in Holocaust memory as a nation that began mass murder *in anticipation* of a Nazi takeover. Hungary learned what the S.S. mobile gassing units were doing in Germany; as a goodwill gesture, the Hungarian state murdered tens of thousands of Hungarian Jews (along with Serbs and others considered "undesirable") in the absence of any suggestion from Berlin and well before the S.S. arrived.

Our continual mandate is to repair and re-create culture in ways that sideline hate, through just laws and just acts. A reason I am foursquare behind marriage equality, for example, is that when the law consistently tells a culture that all its adult citizens are equal, over time people behave more and more as if it's so. That, to a significant extent, is the South's story since school desegregation.

Hate is always present when those with constant, free-floating animus finally find a too-easy target—whether victims of racial, religious, or gender biases, or simply Connecticut six-year-olds. Regardless of its iteration in time, hate confers upon itself a multiplying legitimacy. The unbalanced everywhere take a strange and horrific comfort in incipient and overt hateful acts, no matter how seemingly unrelated or distant. Hate is never lonely; it creates its own zeitgeist.

Acts of justice, small and large, do as well.

Justice is sentient. It exists and it feels. It is also passionate and active when we choose to make it so. It precedes us and outlives us, and instances of it, all our just acts, connect over time and space and powerfully militate toward greater justice, protecting those we love.

Losing Her After Finding Her After the Massacre

1989 - 2013

I am sixty-two; my son is twenty-three.
Ying was our student, our friend, twenty-five on 4 June 1989.
Tian-an-men three thousand dead on the square.
Twenty-six when we bribed her way out of there, when
Tamar and I bribed her way out of there.
She came here, studied, disappeared.
Our son born six months on.

• • •

There have been days, days,
today,
I've told him consequential
inconsequence, meaningful
meaninglessness
more than more than once.

And I ask him about her,
Ying, the one
the China one who's
lost, whom I found and freed, then
lost.

My son is kind, tolerant,

205

holding me in his affectionate eye
all the mornings
I've lamented the same
loss, the same loss
of that new morning.

"Dad."
"I lost her after finding her in that bloody rubble."
"Dad."
"I let her become lost."
"Dad. You got her out."
"And lost. Let her be lost."

Immensely
powerfully made
sequoia of a young man
is this son.

My life's tripwires
come without herald.
No stepping back
across the lines.

I find myself saying again, finding, having found
scores of far-off friends
close friends, early and late,
whom I'd let disappear ages since.

Still Ying's unfound,
remains unfound,
she's the one,
one unfound,
one we spirited from Peking

from the Massacre.
Lost again, she remains unfound.
Lost and I am to blame.

Was it this morning?

Exuberance in finding my found friend
I am imagining or not imagining
having found her not found her
among the many lost
I have found?

Telling my son of her
again again
about her again not twice
this morning
three times
in half an hour
without, by noon,
recall of having said it once, once.

He's not
doubting me.

I ask him have I done
all I could.

Lost.

After she left us in Vermont,
years lost years my
thousand inquiries
London
Cardiff
make a way
be a way
Peking
Xin-Jiang
Waterloo
Thunder Bay
New York
Nowhere

Could have done more.

Have I asked him this
this morning?

He smiles.
He pats my head.

I imagine him
patting.

He says, "Dad.
You will find her."

He pats my head.
He winks.

He rubs my head. He musses my hair.

"Make yourself crazy with this, Dad?
Fine.
The happiest day of the week in the Home is Jello Day."

Reprehensible Writing in Response to the Terror at Boston

2013

The way we use and abuse language speaks to who we are at our cores.

I was put in mind of this as I read and reread, only two days after the bombings in Boston and prior to the identification of the suspects, a half dozen or more posts across a variety of writers' venues using the term *blowback* to describe—as a kind of karma—the attacks on innocent people.

My concerns are these:

- The term was lobbed about by writers who had no evidence whatever but were nonetheless very much hoping the killers represented nations and/or movements with which they have political sympathy—that is, people who have, in their eyes, justice on their side as they strike at civilians here.

- The term is a political cliché that takes no thought or analysis or courage to hurl. It is, in fact, a giving up on analysis on the part of a writer. Using "blowback" and terms like it make it simpler for Left and Right extremists to feel less sickened by a mangled, dead eight-year-old who was, two mornings back, loved by his family. The hundreds of victims remain mangled or dead and loved by their families, while the less-than-they-ought-to-be-sickened writers feel righteous about bloody political struggles which they often appear to write about from a safe distance.

- It and terms like it are used by those who try to mitigate the deaths of innocents by implying that there are no innocents, including children, if a nation has committed bad acts. It's a childish analysis, in fact a "special pleading" kind of analysis, illegitimate (as all "special pleading" is) precisely because every government, whether very or just mildly powerful globally, commits very bad acts. And none of them can remotely justify or bring justice to blown up eight-year-olds or to their families. Even Malcolm X understood at long last that his "chickens come home to roost" explanation of violence was inadequate and ultimately not worthy of himself and his ideals for justice.

It should not be worthy of your own writing or of any writer you read seriously.

The identification of the suspects a few days later didn't stop the Left and Right from speaking foolishly in the wake of the terror at Boston. Even before the pale-as-pale-faced-gets duo was identified, some of the media on the Right had them as Saudi. Others—and here's a shock—had them as black. Even as the fellows' complexions are no longer a matter of tendentious guesswork, the men remain the on-time train for senators hoping for any excuse to derail even modest moves toward immigration justice.

Still, I'm less interested in craven behavior on the Right than I am in sloppy thinking from the Left. I expect more from people I tend to find clearer thinking and better read. Ah, well. The latest iterations of disappointing liberal-left thinking related to the bombings have appeared in numbers of articles and blog posts and are of two types.

Both reduce the killers' motivations to a point of uselessness.

First are writers who want to reduce most, if not all, terrorist behavior to individual psychological maldevelopment. They write as if whatever motivated the Boston brothers is primarily rooted in their personal and emotional backgrounds. Of course, in some cases one can find terrorists whose bad acts can be traced, in part, to prior emotional trauma, abuse, what have you. That may, to a degree, account for those accused of the killings at Newtown, Aurora, Tucson, and, before that, Virginia Tech. (And it's noteworthy that we don't assign "terrorist" to those four.)

But what these writers also do is lump the killers in these incidents with Al Qaeda and similarly affiliated terrorists. I don't think that provides us with an explanation for violence that's of much use, nor do I think it's accurate to suggest that the Newtown and the Aurora shooters as well as those who act as part of organized terror cells and worldwide networks are "of a piece" emotionally. If that idea were translated to counterintelligence practice, we'd be in more, not less, trouble. We know that for many— including the people who attacked us on September 11, 2001—motivation is overwhelmingly religio-political, and whatever part of it may be emotional for individual operatives pales against the dark backdrop of their frankly stated religious and political murderous imperatives.

Moreover, no therapeutic, programmatic "identification and intervention" with committed religio-political terrorist network adherents is possible, even if on some inchoate level, the—to reverse a phrase—"political is personal." Granted: All that we do is in some way personal. That does not mean, however, that it makes sense to speak as if the Newtown killer, the 9/11 conspirators, and the Boston bombers are all "of a piece" and are all susceptible to a similar, discoverable (and, at some time in the past, ameliorable) emotional profile.

A second group of writers also wants to reduce all these bad actors to a single motivation but in a different manner. While some on the liberal-left continuum hope to understand all these murders as instances of psychopathology that we just didn't get to early and effectively enough, others ascribe every contemporary individual and small-group bad act on the world stage to the history of modern geopolitics.

They see the bombings in Boston, for example, as the result of the killers having lived in the violent crucible of Chechen-Russian political, ethnic, and religious conflict. Their subsequent flight to the not-much-more-trustworthy West suggests that we should view their acts not as a result of chosen bad behavior but as a predictable consequence of abstract, largely impersonal, historical forces.

The reason not to accept this line of thinking is clear: Many, many thousands of young people of their generation and origin lived similar lives to theirs and in the same place and also emigrated to the West under the same pressing circumstances and never behaved this way.

Reductive thinking does not do justice to ourselves as writers and citizens, nor does it do justice to victims—or to history.

Afterword: In Dad's Name

Beth Sholom Congregation, Elkins Park, Pennsylvania, is the only synagogue designed by the American architect Frank Lloyd Wright. My sister was a bat mitzvah there and my brother and I were bar mitzvah there. The design reflects Mount Horev (Sinai), where, it is taught, Moses and God met one another. "Beth Sholom" means House of Peace.

Beth Sholom Congregation is also the home for the Bernard Wolfman Civil Discourse Project[1], an annual series of presentations and point/counterpoint discussions on public policy areas of keen current interest. Bernard Wolfman was my father, who died in 2011 at the age of 87. The project was established in his memory by my siblings, my father's wife, and I (primarily through the energies of my remarkable sister, Dina Wolfman Baker).

Dad was a scholar of tax law and legal ethics, known for his teaching of ethics and rules of responsibility for lawyers and for his work in public interest advocacy. After serving in private practice in Philadelphia, he went on to teach at the University of Pennsylvania Law School, where he also served as dean, and at Harvard University Law School.

He was deeply committed to inquiry, thoughtful discussion, and high public and academic standards. He not only practiced law; he sought justice. He saw his work, as I see my writing, as deeply connected to our Jewish heritage and, in particular, to the connection between that heritage and the broader pursuit of justice.

---

[1] http://www.civildiscourseproject.org/

My father expressed this perhaps most poignantly in the remarks he drafted and the action he took when my mother, Zelda Bernstein Wolfman, died in 1973. Dad said, "She was religious in her dedication to the Jewish values of equality and social justice." He went on to establish a fund through which Penn law students can do important work in the area of prisoners' rights—one of my mother's longstanding passions.

The Bernard Wolfman Civil Discourse Project gives both the Jewish and the broader community an opportunity to learn about issues in contemporary American public policy through the following mechanisms:

- Framing the program with an introduction about our father that explores his dual approach of acting assertively, on principle, and proceeding with civility.

- Presenting both sides of an issue through scholars with great expertise in their fields.

- Helping to provide the tools for civil discourse and debate by asking that scholars both teach an issue and model how to engage in passionate and respectful disagreements.

- Ensuring that speakers provide ideas and venues for participants interested in engaging in activism for a particular position.

We hope to hold this forum each year during the intermediate days of *Pesach*/Passover. It's a holiday Dad loved because it brought so many of his family members together and because of the freedom imperatives it reminds us to pursue.

The first program, held on March 28, 2013, focused on the federal government's role in health care. The speakers were Stuart M. Butler, director of the Heritage Foundation's Center for Policy Innovation, and David B. Nash, founder of the Jefferson School of Population Health at Thomas Jefferson University in Philadelphia.

Future forums will focus on topics that include—but are not limited to—immigration; entitlements (societal views of Medicare, Social Security, and personal security); caring for children as a state (public education funding, vouchers, foster care, welfare); state versus federal (where issues such as marriage equality and education belong, and why); theories of U.S. foreign policy; and national food and nutrition policies.

215

The Civil Discourse Project speaks to what my mother and father embodied and taught us at home through their engagement with social issues. They lived, taught, and underscored for me—as evidenced by the moments in my life and work shared in this book—that both in critical, public ethical choice moments and in our smallest, most intimate ones, justice's potential is endlessly transformative. Justice feels and knows those moments and the continual incipient good in every exchange of ideas, in every one of our interactions. Justice waits for us to spark its passion through concerted, tenacious, ongoing creative action, so that it may thrive.

We are most likely to enact justice, make it thrive broadly, when we balance our own serious passion for it with a daily appreciation of this wonderful, wondrous, crazy place we live in, valuing not only the world's seriousness but also its comic, often dark, ironies. We do well to invoke justice daily in our writing, discussion, direct action, and shared laughter.

Justice precedes, outlives, and outdistances us, and all the instances of it created through our just acts connect over time and space and powerfully militate toward a greater good beyond our too-quick moment. Justice asks simply and profoundly that we work to create the necessary conditions to will it as permanent treasure to those we love and to those we'll never know, now, and after we're gone.

North Bethesda, Maryland, April 2013